Parental Perspectives on Care Proceedings

'Studies in Evaluating the Children Act 1989'

Series Editors: Professor Jane Aldgate
Doctor Carolyn Davies

Other titles in the series include
From Care to Accommodation
The Last Resort

STUDIES IN EVALUATING THE CHILDREN ACT 1989

Parental Perspectives on Care Proceedings

Pam Freeman
Joan Hunt

Centre for Socio-Legal Studies
School for Policy Studies, University of Bristol

THE CHILDREN ACT 1989

London: The Stationery Office

First published 1998

ISBN 0 11 322120 7

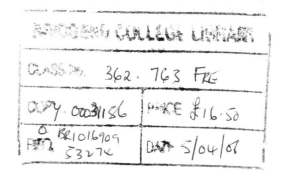

Published by The Stationery Office and available from:

The Publications Centre
(mail, telephone and fax orders only)
PO Box 276, London SW8 5DT
General enquiries 0171 873 0011
Telephone orders 0171 873 9090
Fax orders 0171 873 8200

The Stationery Office Bookshops
123 Kingsway, London WC2B 6PQ
0171 242 6393 Fax 0171 242 6394
68–69 Bull Street, Birmingham B4 6AD
0121 236 9696 Fax 0121 236 9699
33 Wine Street, Bristol BS1 2BQ
0117 926 4306 Fax 0117 929 4515
9–21 Princess Street, Manchester M60 8AS
0161 834 7201 Fax 0161 833 0634
16 Arthur Street, Belfast BT1 4GD
01232 238451 Fax 01232 235401
The Stationery Office Oriel Bookshop
The Friary, Cardiff CF1 4AA
01222 395548 Fax 01222 384347
71 Lothian Road, Edinburgh EH3 9AZ
0131 228 4181 Fax 0131 622 7017

The Stationery Office's Accredited Agents
(see Yellow Pages)

and through good booksellers

Printed in the United Kingdom for The Stationery Office
J62574 10/98 C12 9222

Contents

Acknowledgements   vii

1   Background to the study   1
     The legislative context   1
     The Statutory Intervention Project   2
     The research context: influences on the study   3
     The family context of significant harm   5

2   Methodology   9
     Linkage with the main study: advantages and disadvantages   9
     Research instruments   10
     The access procedure   11
     Access difficulties   12
     The representativeness of the interview sample   14

3   Invoking the court   17
     Unreasonable parenting?   17
     Perspectives on local authority services   20
     The use of accommodation   23
     The need for court action   26
     Participation and partnership   27
     Labelling and stigmatisation   30
     The baggage of negativity   31

4   The court forum   33
     Preparation for court   33
     Waiting at court   35
     Difficulties in attending court   36
     Isolation, exclusion and confusion   37
     In court   38
     Improving the process   44

5   Practitioners in the legal process   48

        Solicitors acting for parents   48

        Barristers   50

        Children's solicitors   51

        The Guardian ad Litem   52

        The judiciary   54

6   The pace of court proceedings   57

        Perceptions of delay   57

        The impact of delay   59

7   The interim period   62

        Interim placements   62

        Interim contact   66

        The need for Interim Contact Orders   69

        The need for Interim Care Orders   70

        Changing circumstances   72

        Participation in welfare decision-making   73

8   The outcome of proceedings   75

        Hopes, fears and realities   75

        Responses to the legal outcome   76

        Parental comprehension of the court's decision   77

        Perceptions of justice   80

        Picking up the pieces   80

9   Summary and ways forward   87

        Summary   87

        Ways forward   92

Bibliography   99

Index   105

Acknowledgements

We are most grateful to the many representatives of local authorities and of other organisations such as the Health, Probation and Prison Services as well as members of the community or voluntary workers who supported the fieldwork. The research was commissioned and funded by the Department of Health and we are also indebted to the members of the Research Advisory Committee, under the chairmanship of Rupert Hughes and later Elizabeth Johnson, for their support and guidance.

Among the contributions from fellow researchers, academics, legal representatives and court officials we would especially like to thank Mervyn Murch, former Director of the Socio-Legal Centre at Bristol University. Dr Jean Packman and Prof. June Thoburn gave us the benefit of their expertise. We would also like to thank Bridget Lindley and members of the Family Rights Group and other parent support groups for their encouragement and advice throughout the research.

Thanks are due also for the support provided by colleagues from the Socio-Legal Centre; to Caroline Thomas, Judith Kent and Pardeep Gill for their preparation of cases and to Maureen Oakley for her data collection. Finally, thanks are owed especially to the administrative team, in particular Doreen Bailey, the Project Administrator, and Rosemary Nash.

We are indebted above all to the family members who participated in the research, without whose help this report could not have been completed. They allowed us into their homes under painful conditions, and shared with us their often distressing experiences. We hope their generosity in contributing their views and criticisms will be rewarded by benefit to others who may encounter the child protection and court system.

Foreword

The Children Act 1989 was implemented on 14 October 1991. At its launch the then Lord Chancellor, Lord MacKay, described the Act as 'the most radical legislative reform to children's services this century'. Shortly after the launch the Department of Health put together a strategy to monitor and evaluate the initial impact of the Act. Taking a tripartite approach, this drew on evidence from statistical returns, inspections and research to develop a rounded appreciation of early implementation. The subsequent strategy plan was published and circulated to relevant bodies, including social services and the major voluntary agencies, in 1993. This plan formed the backcloth for a programme of research studies commissioned by the Department of Health to explore early evaluation in more depth. It is these studies, some 20 in all, which form this new series.

The programme studies investigate the implementation of key changes introduced by the Act and evaluate the facilitators and inhibitors to the meeting of key objectives. A longer-term goal of the programme is to review the aims of the Act in the light of implementation with a view to reconsideration or amendment should this be felt necessary. Finally, a more general and important scientific aim is to consider how far change could be achieved successfully by changing the law.

There are several principles underlying the Children Act 1989 that permeate the research studies. An important strand of the Act is to bring together private and public law so that the needs of all children whose welfare is at risk might be approached in the same way. This philosophy is underpinned by the principle of promoting children's welfare. There should be recognition of children's time-scales and, in court cases, children's welfare should be paramount. To aid this paramountcy principle there should be a welfare checklist and delays in court hearings should be avoided.

The promotion of children's welfare takes a child development focus, urging local authorities to take a holistic and corporate approach to providing services. Departments such as health, education, housing, police, social services and recreation should work together to respond to children's needs. Children, the Act argues, are best looked after within their families wherever possible and, where not, the continuing support of parents and wider kin should be facilitated by avoiding compulsory proceedings whenever possible. Parents should be partners in any intervention process, and children's views should be sought and listened to in any decision-making affecting their lives. To promote continuity for children looked after, contact with families should be encouraged and children's religion, culture ethnicity and language should be preserved.

Local authorities have a duty to move from services to prevent care to a broader remit of providing family support, which could include planned periods away from home. However, family support services should not be universal but target those most in need. The introduction of Children's Services Plans in 1996 has made the idea of corporate responsibility a more tangible reality and seeks to help local authorities look at how they may use scarce resources cost effectively.

The themes of the Children Act have relevance for the millennium. The concern with combating social exclusion is echoed through several of the studies, especially those on family support and young people looked after by local authorities. The value of early intervention is also a theme in the studies on family centres, day care and services for children defined as 'in need' under the Act. Further, the research on the implementation of the Looking After Children Schedules emphasises the importance to children in foster and residential care of attaining good outcomes in education. Lastly, attending to the health of parents and their children is another strand in both the family support and 'children looked after' studies.

To accompany the 20 individual studies in the research programme the Department of Health has commissioned an overview of the findings, to be published by The Stationery Office in the style of similar previous publications from HMSO: *Social Work Decisions in Child Care 1985; Pattern and Outcomes in Child Care 1991; Child Protection: Messages from Research 1996;* and *Focus on Teenagers 1997.*

The editors would like to express their appreciation to the members of the research community, professionals from different disciplines, and service users, among others, who have contributed so willingly and generously to the successful completion of the research studies and to the construction of the overview. Without their help, none of the research would have been written or disseminated.

Jane Aldgate
Carolyn Davies

1 *Background to the study*

The legislative context

The ethos of the Children Act 1989 is profoundly familial and voluntaristic. As the highly influential official introductory guide to the new legislation stressed:

> It rests on the belief that children are generally best looked after within the family and with both parents playing a full part and without resort to legal proceedings.[1]

Even where parental care is called into question the Act strives to provide a 'better balance' between the need to protect children from failures or abuse within the family and the harm caused by unwarranted state interference. Statutory intervention is to be the last resort.[2] Families are to be helped wherever possible by the provisions of services. Where this is no longer possible and the local authority acquires legal powers over a child, parental responsibility is not transferred but merely shared. The duty to work in partnership with parents, which begins when the first contact is made with the family, does not cease, although it may, it is admitted, become more difficult to achieve.[3]

The Children Act was passed after a long and complex gestation: conceived out of dissatisfaction with fragmented legislation,[4] shaped by thorough reviews of the public and private law relating to children,[5] nourished by a series of public inquiries into child deaths[6] and an extensive programme of research into child care services.[7] The emphasis in the Act upon the protection of family autonomy, and the negative effects of state intervention, however, acquired a sharp resonance in the light of events in Cleveland in 1987. The allegations of widespread but hitherto unsuspected familial sexual abuse, the precipitate removal of hundreds of children, usually on Place of Safety Orders against which there was no right of appeal, the denial of access and information to parents and the breakdown of interagency co-operation, prompted a long and high profile enquiry which attracted an entirely new level of public attention, fed by daily media coverage. The resultant highly influential Report[8] drew attention not only to the dilemmas surrounding child protection but to the confusion, anger and distress of parents caught up in the processes of investigation and the way in which their legitimate interests had been trampled on throughout.

Thus, though the welfare of the child is the paramount concern of the court in determining children's cases,[9] the Act provides significant new legislative safeguards against unwarranted intervention combined with improved mechanisms for the expression and protection of parental interests. At the same time, in a parallel development which had also received considerable stimulation from research, there was a new emphasis on the need for social services departments to work in a more participatory way with parents.[10]

Most families are involved in the child protection system relatively briefly[11] and compulsory removal of children from home is thankfully not a commonplace experience[12] – although even coming under a suspicion of abuse can be an uncomfortable or sometimes devastating experience.[13] The research reported here is concerned with the tiny proportion of families at the other end of the continuum where all preventative resources appear to have failed or a dramatic incident of abuse catapults them into the court process. It examines the extent to which the new emphasis on working with families is reflected in the experiences of the parents who are unwilling but key players in the legal process.

The Statutory Intervention Project

The research documented in this report was one strand of a project evaluating the impact of the Children Act on the use of the courts in child protection.[14] This involved urban areas in three local authorities and the courts which they feed and included both a pre- and post-Act dimension. The other main elements in this study have been:

- a large statistical survey of cases involving care and related proceedings starting in the magistrates' courts in the two years before and two years after the Act;
- a detailed examination of court and local authority files in 83 post-Act cases brought in care proceedings and in 104 care, wardship or matrimonial proceedings pre-Act;
- observation of court hearings in 30 post-Act cases;
- interviews with around 150 practitioners (social workers, team managers, Guardians ad Litem and lawyers acting for local authority, children or parents) involved in a selection of the 83 post-Act cases; and

- general interviews with judges, district judges, magistrates and justices' clerks.

The research findings from these strands of the project have been reported separately.[15] The primary emphasis of this element in the research has been on exploring the quality and nature of parents' experiences through an analysis of their self-reported perspectives. It draws on, illuminates and often confirms the findings of the parallel study while also raising different issues and viewpoints. In some respects, of course, parental accounts may be felt to be distorted or biased and certainly at times they were inconsistent with other information available to the research team. Where these differences appear to be significant they have been highlighted. We have sought to achieve a balance between uncritically accepting parental reports as the unvarnished truth and denying the reality of their experiences by explaining them away. It is rare for different actors in an interactive experience to give precisely the same account even in the discourse of daily life. We need only think of reports made to the media or the police following a tragic event such as a road accident or a disaster to demonstrate that there may be as many versions of the story as there are witnesses.

The research context: influences on the study

Socio-legal influences

Exploration of the litigant perspective in family law has been a key component in the Socio-Legal Centre's research since its inception.[16] This study builds upon that tradition and draws specifically on unpublished work relating to parents' experiences of care proceedings in the juvenile court of ten years ago, conducted in the course of research into the implementation of the provisions for separate representation.[17] That study provided a unique baseline against which to evaluate the extent to which the ideals of the Children Act were reflected in the experiences of families.

In developing the research instrument it was of course invaluable to be able to incorporate the insights of other members of the full research team. We were also able to have a mutually beneficial contact with the Family Rights Group who were setting up their parallel research[18] into families' experiences of the court process at the same time, ensuring a degree of harmonisation of the research questions. Since fieldwork on other aspects of the Statutory Intervention Project was revealing that members of the extended family were playing an increasing role in care proceedings under the Act, we sought to interview a small number of non-parent relatives who were made parties to proceedings, drawing particularly upon a report on custodianship by our colleagues Malos and Bullard,[19] and on children placed home on trial by Farmer and Parker,[20] both studies which employed a wider family perspective.

All these studies helped to focus this research and to identify a range of topics for investigation, from practical aspects of the court process (such as the environment, accessibility, facilities for children) to professional input, quality of information, advice and representation, participation, and crucially – although most nebulous of all – the degree to which adult family members felt they had experienced justice.

Other questions to be addressed were drawn from work on delay in the legal process,[21] reframing new ideas from New Zealand and Australia about the involvement of the extended family in decision-making in child protection[22] and older ideas about court fora from Scotland[23] and the Family Courts Campaign. Most central were key concepts in the Act itself as identified in official guidance, particularly the themes of partnership and participation.

Influences of child care research

The study also fits into a well-established tradition of research into the perspectives of those in receipt of welfare services beginning with the seminal work of Timms[24] and more recently those of Browne and Corby.[25] Most relevant to our present purposes has been the large programme of research into child protection commissioned by the Department of Health (DoH) in the wake of Cleveland, which has now come to fruition.[26] Many of these studies either specifically focus upon or incorporate a user dimension and have provided pertinent insights into the way child protection services are perceived by families.[27]

As indicated earlier, the findings of that research programme demonstrate that the majority of families referred to child protection agencies because of allegations of abuse or neglect are filtered out of the system relatively rapidly with few cases being case-conferenced and even fewer registered. It was therefore entirely appropriate that the research programme should concentrate upon the early stages of intervention affecting large numbers of families, rather than court action which is relevant to only a small minority. None the less the absence of even a single study dealing with the legal process was a notable gap.

At the other end of the spectrum from the DoH research programme we also took account of a report by the pressure group PAIN[28] on the experiences of

30 parents who claimed to have been falsely accused of child abuse. As we shall see, although the PAIN sample were perhaps more vociferous about the perceived injustices of a system they felt to have been judgemental and stigmatising from the outset, many of their unhappy experiences were echoed by families participating in our research.

It was a fundamental principle of the Bristol study that it should avoid an overly narrow focus upon the child protection aspects of the cases but should integrate these with the families' broader experiences of the whole socio-legal process. We therefore incorporated into the research design insights from the body of knowledge on care careers and family links,[29] examining parental perspectives on areas of potential conflict between family and agency, the nature and quality of contact, interim placements, separation and return of children. Anticipating that a significant proportion of our case families would lose their children to permanent substitute care we also drew on the wide body of literature dealing with permanency planning and adoption.[30] We were fortunate in forging links with the Natural Parent Group whose informal input about the feelings and experiences of birth parents whose children had been adopted gave us much insight and helped to contextualise the experiences of the case families.

The family context of significant harm

In taking the decision to seek statutory powers under the Children Act in child protection cases the local authority has to be reasonably confident that it can satisfy the court:

- that the child is suffering or is likely to suffer significant harm [Section 31 (2)(a)];
- that harm, or its likelihood is attributable to the care given, or likely to be given, not being what it would be reasonable to expect a parent to give to him [Section 31 (2)(b)(i)];
- that the order sought is better for the child than making no order at all [Section 1 (5)]; and
- that the order will be in the child's interests as defined in the welfare checklist [Sections 1 (1) and 1 (3)].

These formidable obstacles mean that court action is not likely to be taken unless there is serious concern about the quality of parenting and other means of dealing with that concern are considered to be inappropriate or to have already failed.[31] Moreover, while there will be a significant minority of cases which do not result in a public law order, the findings of the main study also show that this is almost always because of changes in the family situation which make alternative remedies feasible, and very rarely because the allegations of significant harm are not proven. In undertaking research into the parental perspective in these cases it is crucial not to deny that reality.

It is equally crucial, however, to acknowledge the major problems with which the parents involved in these highly problematic and apparently intractable cases are struggling: social exclusion in the form of poverty or poor housing; mental illness, substance misuse, domestic violence, and their own experiences of inadequate parenting, abuse and public care. In addition to the extensive literature on the aetiology of child abuse[32] we have drawn upon research dealing with particular areas of vulnerability, notably families where there is mental illness,[33] learning disabilities[34] and family violence.[35]

NOTES

[1] Department of Health (1989): *An Introduction to the Children Act 1989*. HMSO.

[2] Department of Health (1992):*The Children Act 1989 Court Orders Study*, SSI; Department of Health (1989): *The Care of Children (1989): Principles and Practice in Guidance and Regulations*. HMSO; Department of Health (1991): *Working Together Under the Children Act 1989*. HMSO; Department of Health (1991): *Patterns and Outcomes in Child Placement*. HMSO.

[3] DoH/SSI (1995): *The Challenge of Partnership in Child Protection: Practice Guide*. HMSO.

[4] Second Report from the Social Services Committee (1984): HC 360. HMSO.

[5] DHSS (1985): *Review of Child Care Law: Report to Ministers of an Interdepartmental Working Party*; Law Commission (1988): *Family Law: Review of Child Law: Guardianship and Custody*. Law Comm no 172. HMSO.

[6] Notably London Borough of Brent (1985): *A Child in Trust: Report of the Panel of Inquiry Investigating the Circumstances Surrounding the Death of Jasmine Beckford*. Kingswood Press; London Borough of Lambeth (1987): *Whose Child? the Report of the Public Inquiry into the Death of Tyra Henry*; London Borough of Greenwich (1987): *A Child in Mind: Protection of Children in a Responsible Society: Report of the Commission of Inquiry into the Circumstances Surrounding the Death of Kimberley Carlile*.

[7] DHSS (1985): *Social Work Decisions in Child Care*. HMSO; Dartington Social Research Unit (1995): *Child Protection and Child Abuse: Messages from Research*; Department of Health: *Studies in Child Protection*. HMSO.

[8] DHSS (1988): *Report of the Inquiry into Child Abuse in Cleveland 1987*. Cm 412, HMSO.

[9] Children Act 1989, Section 1 (1).

[10] Thoburn J; Lewis A; Shemmings D (1995): *Paternalism or Partnership? Family Involvement in the Child Protection Process*; Department of Health: *Studies in Child Protection*; Social Services Inspectorate (1995): *The Challenge of Partnership in Child Protection*.

[11] Gibbons J; Conroy S; Bell C (1995): *Operating the Child Protection System*. HMSO.

[12] Around 160,000 children are subject to child protection investigations under Section 47 of the Children Act every year, 96% remain at home and the majority of those separated are swiftly returned. DoH (1995): *Child Protection: Messages from Research*. HMSO. According to Gibbons et al. (1995) *op. cit.* only 4% of children investigated were removed from home under a legal order during the investigation.

[13] Cleaver H; Freeman P (1995): *Parental Perspectives in Cases of Suspected Child Abuse*. Department of Health Studies in Child Protection. HMSO.

[14] *Statutory Intervention in Child Protection: the Impact of the Children Act 1989*. For simplicity, the other elements in this project are referred to throughout this Report as the '*main study*'.

[15] Hunt J; Macleod A (1999): *The Last Resort: Child Protection, the Courts and the 1989 Children Act*. The Stationery Office. Thomas C; Hunt J (1996): *The Case Workloads of the Civil Courts under the Children Act*. Research Report, Centre for Socio-Legal Studies, University of Bristol.

[16] For example: *Marital Violence, the Community Response* (1983); *Special Procedure in Divorce* (1983); *Access after Divorce* (1984); *Overlapping Jurisdiction of County and Magistrates' Courts in Family Business* (1985); *Representation of the Child in the Civil Courts* (1990).

[17] *Representation of the Child in the Civil Courts* research project, 1985–90.

[18] Lindley B (1994): *On the Receiving End*. Family Rights Group.

[19] Malos E; Bullard E (1991): *Custodianship: Caring for Other People's Children*. HMSO.

[20] Farmer E; Parker R (1991): *Trials and Tribulations: Returning Children from Local Authority Care to their Families*. HMSO.

[21] Murch M; Mills E (1987): *The Length of Care Proceedings*. Socio-Legal Centre for Family Studies, University of Bristol. Masson J; Morton S (1989): 'The use of wardship by local authorities'. *Modern Law Review*, November 1989. Hunt J (1993): *Local Authority Wardships before the Children Act: the Baby or the Bathwater?* HMSO. Plotnikoff J; Woolfson R (1994): *The Timetabling of Interim Care Orders: a Study Carried out on Behalf of the Social Services Inspectorate*. HMSO.

[22] Tunnard J (ed) (1994): *Family Group Conferences: a Report Commissioned by the Department of Health*. Family Rights Group/DoH.

[23] Scottish Office (1993): *Scotland's Children: Proposals for Child Care Policy and Law*. HMSO.

[24] Mayer J; Timms N (1970): *The Client Speaks: Working-Class Impressions of Casework*. Routledge Kegan Paul.

[25] Browne C (1986): *Child Abuse: Parents Speaking. Impressions of Social Workers and the Social Work Process*. Bristol University School of Advanced Urban Studies. Corby B (1987): *Working with Child Abuse: Social Work Practice and the Child Abuse System*. Oxford University Press.

[26] DoH (1995): *op. cit.*

[27] Notably: Cleaver; Freeman (1995) *op. cit.* Farmer E; Owen M (1995): *Child Protection Practice: Private Risks and Public Remedies*. HMSO.

[28] Prosser P (1992): *Child Abuse Investigations: the Families' Perspective*. Commissioned and published by PAIN – Parents Against Injustice.

[29] Milham S; Bullock R; Hosie K; Haak M (1986): *Lost in Care: the Problems of Maintaining Links between Children in Care and their Families*. Gower. Milham S; Bullock R; Hosie K; Little M (1989): *Access Disputes in Child Care*. Gower. Rowe J; Cain H; Hundleby M; Keane A (1984): *Long-Term Foster Care*. Batsford. Bullock R; Little M; Milham S (1993): *Going Home*. Dartmouth Press. Berridge D; Cleaver H (1987): *Foster Home Breakdown*. Blackwell.

[30] For example: Howe D; Sawbridge P; Hinings D (1992): *Half a Million Women: Mothers who Lose their Children by Adoption*. Penguin. Borkowski M; Copner R; Lowe N (1993): *Pathways to Adoption*. HMSO. DoH (1995): *Looking after Children; Review of Arrangements for a Child or Young Person looked after by a Local Authority*. Department of Health.

[31] Hunt; Macleod (1999): *op. cit.*

[32] Browne K; Davies C; Stratton P (1988): *Early Prediction and Prevention of Child Abuse*. Wiley. Quinton D; Rutter M (1988): *Parenting Breakdown: Making and Breaking of Intergenerational Links*. Gower. Garbarino J; Gilliam S (1980): *Understanding Abusive Families*. Lexington Books. Waterhouse L (1992): *Child Abuse and Child Abusers*. Jessica Kingsley.

[33] Weir A (1994): '"Split decisions": child care: how adult mental health affects children'. *Community Care*, 1.12.94. Isaac BC; Minty EB; Morrison RM (1986): 'Children in care – the association with mental disorder in the parents'. *British Journal of Social Work*, Vol 16, no 3. Hugman R; Phillips N (1994): 'Like bees round the honeypot: social work responses to parents with mental health needs'. *Practice*, Vol 6, no 3. Feldman et al. (1987): *Children at Risk – the Web of Mental Illness*. Rutgers University Press.

[34] Turner S; Sweeney D; Hayes L (1994): *Developments in Community Care for Adults with Learning Disabilities: a Review of 1993/4 Community Care Plans*. University of Manchester. Conley PW; Luckasen R; Bouthilet GM (eds) (1992): *The Criminal Justice System and Mental Retardation – Defendants and Victims*. Paul H Brookes Publishing Co.

[35] Hester M; Radford L (1995): *Domestic Violence and Child Care Arrangements in England and Denmark*. The Policy Press. Gelles RJ (1987): *Family Violence*. (2nd edition). Sage Library of Social Research, California.

2 *Methodology*

Linkage with the main study: advantages and disadvantages

Negotiating such a sensitive research area, we knew from experience,[1] would not be easy. However there were several benefits we hoped would accrue from the linkage of the parent interviews to a larger project. It was anticipated that the sample would consist largely of parents who had agreed to researchers observing their case in court. They would thus have already received information about the research and had an opportunity to discuss it with their solicitors as well as with the researchers. In a number of cases consent in principle to interviews once proceedings were complete had been obtained.

Much of the essential groundwork had already been done in establishing the main study: consent from the local authorities and courts involved had been obtained, ethical issues addressed and many of the relevant practitioners were familiar with the research, having been contacted, and in some cases already interviewed. Although it was unnecessary to seek permission from Social Services before approaching parents, we considered it was courteous and sensitive to inform social workers when we were doing this. In fact we found them to be extremely helpful and assiduous in smoothing the way to contact.

By the time we made the first approach to parents information from case files had already been collated. Although there are arguments for interviewing blind this was not logistically possible because some of the researchers were involved in both studies. We therefore decided to exploit fully the available information and inform parents that we were familiar with the case papers.

These data proved to be extremely useful in focusing the interviews and sensitising the researchers to any areas likely to be particularly painful for parents to discuss. It also allowed a certain amount of background and quantitative data to be incorporated in the research analysis which would not have been otherwise possible.

The disadvantages of the linkage between the two studies however were that we could not extend the sampling pool, and the timing of interviews was determined by the pace of the court proceedings. The target duration of care proceedings under the Act was initially 12 weeks; in reality the average duration of cases in the study was around six months with a few lasting much longer than this. Thus it was necessary both to reduce the size of the projected sample and to extend the length of the project, although this did allow us to take account of the greater involvement of members of the extended family. It was also possible to conduct a few repeat interviews when this proved necessary and to respond to the desire of quite a few of the families interviewed early in the research to keep us informed of subsequent developments. It was partly as a result of issues raised by these contacts that the research team subsequently obtained funding from the DoH for a new study examining the implementation of court decisions.[2]

Such continuing contact served to confirm that although the interviewing process was often extremely painful for parents it was also, as they often told us, a positive experience for them. However, it also reflects the desperate need some parents had for post-proceedings support, particularly those who were facing up to the permanent loss of their children, a point to which we shall return.

Research instruments

Interviews were face-to-face and semi-structured. In designing a research schedule for parents we found it helpful to consult instruments developed by other researchers working in this field as well as those we had previously utilised. It was also valuable to have comment from members of our Project Advisory Group, which included representatives of practitioner groups, relevant government departments, the judiciary and fellow researchers. Careful and time-consuming preparation of the research schedules ensured that we had a selection of simply worded but probing questions which could be adapted appropriately and flexibly to interview parents with learning difficulties or mental illness or those whose first language was not English as well as parents from more advantaged backgrounds. Working on the basis of this instrument we were then able to design a second schedule with which to interview members of the extended family.

Where possible interviews were transcribed in full to assist the process of analysis. Quotations from the transcripts are used throughout the report. Only three families proved reluctant to be taped although one aggressive father walked in on an interview to which his wife had consented, and quite calculatedly destroyed one side of the recording on a pretence that he was showing the tape-recorder to his child. Another interview did not begin for an hour, while the researcher and mother assessed the risk of violence from her husband if she were to be caught confiding her thoughts. In the event, the mother decided to risk any repercussions and the interview eventually lasted six hours!

Time was also well spent training the original team of three researchers in the use of the research instruments and interviewing techniques, particularly those involving minority groups, and discussing ethical issues around consent, intrusion or disclosure as well as other practical issues which might arise in the course of the fieldwork stage, although because of delay in the completion of cases, only two of the original researchers completed interviews. The parity of the research data acquired by each gave us some confidence in the chosen methodology and the research tools, while the similarity of the findings in all three research areas suggests that the experiences of our small sample of case families have a more general applicability.

In view of our concern for the safety of the women researchers visiting often unsafe locations at night, the researchers were equipped with mobile phones which thankfully were not required to be used in an emergency. Provision was also made for the use of escorts where a household included a potentially violent adult. Although this approach ultimately proved unnecessary both were important precautions to build into a research project of this nature.

The access procedure

Our final interview sample consisted both of parents who were aware of the research because they had consented to us attending their proceedings and those who knew nothing at all about it. Two initial letters therefore had to be designed, and great care taken with those which would be received cold. Provision was made for translating into a range of non-European languages.

In all cases, before any approach was made, we contacted the key social worker (and on occasion other relevant practitioners, including hospital or prison staff, health workers or probation officers) to discuss the feasibility of the research interview. As we have already indicated most of those engaged in this manner proved very helpful and we acknowledge their very effective assistance. Difficulties in actually making contact with practitioners, however, undoubtedly slowed down the access process as we fell victim to leave, meetings, training courses, illnesses and pregnancies, changes of worker, unallocated cases or no clear lines of case management, in addition to the commitments of workers to heavy caseloads. The telephone bill was stupendous! The frustrations voiced by parents that their social workers were never available did not fall on deaf ears while our experience of abortive visits makes us sympathise with workers who complained that their clients were never there either.

Contact with practitioners, when eventually made, was used to complete a checklist about the current circumstances of the family. This included their present whereabouts, any changes in the household, any further incidents of abuse or concurrent criminal or civil proceedings and the need for any special interview arrangements such as an interpreter. This procedure effectively served several purposes: it provided up-to-date information on the case families, served as a focus for gaining co-operation and support from practitioners, and helped to filter out potentially unsuitable case families from the research so that we did not waste effort on doubtful visits.

We were very clear in our own minds that in liaising with the social worker we were not seeking permission to approach parents and fortunately it never became necessary to make that explicit. However we did on occasion agree to postpone contact if the social worker considered the time was particularly inapposite, for example if there was a contested adoption in process or a parent's mental health was particularly unstable. In this way we sought to avoid the risk of rocking the boat or increasing parental distress.

On satisfactory completion of this process, an initial letter of introduction was sent, unless the case had been recently finalised and a parent had already consented. The letter explained the nature of the research, reminded parents of any earlier contact (for example, the name of the researcher who had attended their case) and explained about confidentiality and anonymity.[3] A formal refusal slip with a stamped addressed envelope was enclosed. Parents were asked to reply within seven days of receipt and alerted to the fact that if they did not reply we would assume they were willing to participate and would send a provisional appointment. This approach was selected on the basis of previous experience, namely that very few interviews can be achieved if positive notification of consent is required. Parents were given a second chance to refuse by means of a second letter giving a provisional appointment.

Although only nine parents used the refusal slip, when they did the response was very prompt, indicating how adamant they felt. One or two also either phoned the Centre directly or had a trusted practitioner do so on their behalf.

Access difficulties

Forty-four families were eventually contacted and at least one interview conducted in 25, adding up to a total of 34 family members. In one case alone the researcher interviewed five different family members who were all anxious that their mutually antagonistic viewpoints should be heard.

The success rate varied considerably between the three study areas. In area B 90% of approaches resulted in an interview compared with 55% in area A and 39% in area C. The remarkably high rate in area B, where the researcher conducting the family interviews had also been present at most of the hearings, we thought must be at least partly explained by continuity.[4] Awareness of the research *per se* was no guarantee of success since we had seven refusals from parents in the observed sample who had previously told the researcher attending court that they were willing to be interviewed. Conversely we were able to interview nine families from 'cold'.

Timing of the approach appeared to be an important factor in its success, although it was very difficult to judge what *was* the right time since it seemed to vary between families. We had refusals in recently completed cases where parents said they were still too raw from the experience and in those where months had elapsed and parents did not want to revisit the distress they were trying to put behind them. Sometimes it seemed the research created its own momentum and parents contacted us months later saying they were now ready to be interviewed.

A more critical aspect may have been what else was going on in the parents' lives at the time. It was often necessary to proceed much more slowly than we would ideally have wished, perhaps because children were being rehabilitated or a parent was preoccupied with adoption or contact proceedings. Some parents had new partners who may not have been fully aware of the circumstances of the case; some sadly had been admitted or readmitted to psychiatric hospital; others were involved in intensive programmes of assessment or treatment. A few could not be tracked down. One chronically drug-addicted mother, for instance, disappeared shortly after the final court hearing at which she conceded the Care Order and despite the efforts of a whole range of agencies, including Social Services, who were anxious to proceed with adoption, was lost to sight, generating considerable concerns for her safety. Six months later she reappeared, no longer taking drugs and with a new partner and a new home many miles away.

A more common problem, however, was parents who did not formally refuse to be interviewed but were persistently not at home, a scenario with which researchers and practitioners alike will be familiar. Many a coffee was drunk in a dingy cafe on a cold winter day or time spent on a park bench in a shady part of a city, waiting to see if a parent would return! In order to give parents the benefit of the doubt, we left notes explaining we would call back in an hour or so and on occasion this proved successful. On others the note had disappeared but so had the parent. In some cases we were fairly certain some-one was in the house but not answering the door. After a while we abandoned the time-consuming practice of repeat visits unless there was some evidence of a failure of communication, accepting reluctantly that if parents wanted to be interviewed they would generally keep the appointment and if not they would vote with their feet.

Untraceable parents and passive refusal were particularly a feature of cases in area C. This is almost certainly not unrelated to the higher proportion of sample parents in this area addicted to drugs or alcohol or suffering from psychiatric illness. Despite a small extension to the fieldwork phase which enabled approaches to be made to a further six families in this area these all proved unsuccessful. Most disappointing was a mother in a psychiatric hospital who at the time of the court case had *asked* to be interviewed. After a very careful process of negotiation first with social work and then medical staff, an interview was arranged, but at the last minute mother could not face it and left the ward.

The interview sample slightly over-represents families with a parent from an ethnic minority group: 44% compared to 39% in the sample overall. However, we were particularly disappointed that though some Asian families agreed to be interviewed, our success rate with this group, especially with Sikh families, was very low, despite the fact we were able to offer a Punjabi-speaking researcher from outside the local communities.[5]

Two other groups also seemed to be more reluctant to be interviewed. We had a particularly low strike rate (1 in 11) with families new to the child pro-tection system, who had usually been catapulted into court via an Emergency Protection Order. It also seemed that families whose children had been returned home were less likely to agree to see us. We can only speculate why this may be; it is possible either that they were more satisfied with their case outcome and therefore had less reason to want to express their views, or that they were anxious not to do anything which might rock the boat. The inter-views we did manage to achieve with parents in this situation suggested it was more likely to be the latter.

The representativeness of the interview sample

As a result of these factors the interview sample cannot claim to be fully representative even of the main sample and therefore we make no claim that the views described in the subsequent pages can be taken as typical of all the parents passing through the court process. The families subject to care proceedings are ranged along a continuum. At one end is a small minority whose first contact with the child protection system produces legal action, usually as the result of some dramatic incident or allegation. At the other is another, larger, minority who are not only well known to child protection agencies but have been previously subject to compulsory intervention. In the middle are the bulk of cases who have already become caught up in local authority protection processes and may even have been considered for court on several occasions but are crossing the Rubicon for the first time.

The interview sample consists essentially of these latter two groups. Ninety-two per cent of families, for instance, were already being worked with prior to any events precipitating proceedings. Seventy-two per cent of cases had been active for more than three months and 56% for more than a year. In 64% of cases at least one of the case children was already on the Child Protection Register and 32% had children not subject to the sample proceedings who were already being looked after by the local authority. In 20% of cases at least one of the case children had been subject to previous proceedings and 40% had experienced separation from their parents. All of these figures are higher than those for the total sample.

Consistent with this picture of a group of families whose parenting has been under scrutiny for some considerable time we found that the interview cases were less likely than the sample as a whole to arrive in court as the result of a crisis or to be subject to compulsory emergency protection (32% compared with around 46% of the main sample), although the proportion living at home prior to proceedings (52%) was almost identical. This is undoubtedly due, at least in part, to the fact that the concerns leading to court action in the interview sample were more likely to involve neglect or emotional ill-treatment (56%) than physical or sexual abuse (40%). While this was also true of the sample as a whole the difference was smaller (5%).

The characteristics and circumstances of the interview families also diverged slightly. They were, for example, more likely to have at least two children sub-ject to proceedings and to have other, non-case children. The case children tended to be slightly younger: the mean age of the eldest child in each case for instance being 4.2 years compared with 4.7, and the youngest 2.6 years compared with 3.1.

Despite the fact that these were, in general, families who had attracted the concern of state agencies over often lengthy periods, the interview sample exhibited slighter lower levels of what might be regarded as social morbidity than the main sample. Slightly fewer of the adults had been abused or in care as children themselves. Parents were less likely to be attempting to bring up children without a partner and fewer mothers had had their first child at a very early age. More of the households contained someone in employment and fewer an adult with a criminal record. Rates for domestic violence, mental illness, substance abuse and learning disability were all lower than for the families overall.

Some of the differences, however, were very slight and with the exception of mental illness (9%) not more than 5%. Most of the parents interviewed were struggling with the same range of adverse circumstances described in our parallel research report *The Last Resort* [6] – low incomes, specific impediments to parenting as a result of illness, disability or addiction, violent partnerships and poor experiences of parenting themselves. It is hard to imagine a group less well-equipped to participate on an equal footing in the complex and highly professionalised legal system into which they had been hurled by their perceived parenting deficiencies. Before turning to what our interviewees had to say about their experiences with the legal system we look at their perspective on the processes which led to the local authority applying for a court order.

NOTES

[1] All the researchers involved in the study had experience of conducting similar research. The difficulties which can be encountered are also described in Cleaver H; Freeman P (1995): *Parental Perspectives in Cases of Suspected Child Abuse*. HMSO.

[2] Hunt J; Macleod A (forthcoming): *The Best-Laid Plans: the Outcomes of Judicial Decision-Making*. The Stationery Office.

[3] *Personal Social Services: Confidentiality of Personal Information*. LAC (88) 17 DoH (1988).

[4] We are starting to question this finding from similar experiences in the *Best-Laid Plans* study, however, where again the success rate in area B was high, despite the use of an unfamiliar researcher.

[5] Kadushin A (1972): 'The racial factor in the interview'. *Social Work*, Vol 17, no 3, pp 88–97.

[6] Hunt J; Macleod A (1999): *The Last Resort: Child Protection, the Courts and the 1989 Children Act*. The Stationery Office.

3 *Invoking the court*

Unreasonable parenting?

In the vast majority of our sample cases, as demonstrated in the previous chapter, there had been official concerns over the quality of parental care for a substantial period. There had often been a *career* of suspicion resulting in escalating levels of monitoring, while 64% of families had had children on the Child Protection Register, indicating that their children were deemed to be at risk of significant harm. Moreover while a proportion of cases did not result in a public law order none failed because the threshold criteria were not met. Thus after due process of law, in which the matter was thoroughly aired before an independent tribunal with full rights of representation, the children in this study were deemed to have suffered or to be at risk of suffering significant harm attributable to the quality of their parenting.[1] Yet 83% of the parents, all interviewed after proceedings had been completed, continued to deny, either in full or in part, the nature or the severity of the concerns which had resulted in court action.

Courts, of course, as has been only too apparent in recent years, are by no means infallible, even when the standard of proof required, as in the criminal courts, is very tough. High profile scandals such as Cleveland and Orkney demonstrate that welfare agencies can act precipitately while organisations such as PAIN owe their existence to allegations of miscarriages of justice. There are also much wider philosophical and moral questions about the possibility of legal justice in an unjust society – questions which have a disturbing resonance in the context of these generally very deprived families. Within the parameters of our existing system, however, it is simply not credible that the process went wrong in so many of our sample cases. It is therefore necessary to look elsewhere to explain such discrepant perspectives.

It is well established that the test of reasonable parenting is not a matter of assessing culpability but an objective evaluation of parenting standards. For instance, a parent may earnestly wish to do the best for his/her child but be prevented from doing so by virtue of psychiatric illness. To introduce this into the equation however, the rationale goes, would result in the acceptance of lower standards of care for children of disadvantaged parents.

Such subtleties, which may on occasion be difficult even for professionals to appreciate,[2] are likely to be of little import to parents. Indeed, we suggest, it would be a rare person who, faced with allegations that his/her parenting falls short of community standards, would not feel to some degree blamed or see the process as anything other than a shaming experience.

The coping strategies we all on occasion employ to protect our self-esteem, which in many of the parents in this study was particularly fragile, have been well described by Matza and Sykes.[3] Of particular interest is the work of Abel and Becker's[4] research on self-reporting perpetrators of sexual offences and the literature on reactions to stress or bereavement.[5] Techniques such as denial, shifting the blame, minimisation and justification were all evident in many of the research interviews, sometimes within the same interchange. This point is illustrated by one father's response when asked whether he thought Social Services' concerns were valid:

> A lot of it was exaggerated. Every time we have a problem with Social Services when we tell them we don't want them coming round any more it always seems after that we have trouble. One time it was bruising, another time it was that he was hungry, neglecting him and we've got to look after him. There is no hungriness [sic] in him and we have got other youngsters to feed as well, exactly the same.

Here we observe the seriousness of official concerns being minimised, the blame being shifted onto an intrusive and victimising social services department and simultaneously both the charge of neglect denied and behaviour which might be construed as neglect justified.

As explained earlier, the parents we interviewed were made aware from the outset that the researchers were familiar with the details of their case. The extent of the denial of significant harm to the child was therefore all the more striking. For example, two mothers did not make a single reference in the course of very lengthy interviews to the allegations of serious sexual or physical abuse (even though as a result their partners were serving terms of imprisonment), choosing to focus upon perhaps more acceptable concerns. One told us:

> It was about my son [aged five] who kept running off. He was out of control.

Other parents blamed their partners, especially those who had been mentally ill, were substance abusers or had a history of sexual abuse. Where the couple were still together it was evident that recriminations had continued to dog family life long after the court proceedings had ended:

> The blaming started between us, because my husband drank more than me, but they came down heavy on me and I felt very bitter and insulted that they didn't recognise this and it all focused on me and I couldn't tell them how it was, which was half and half. I felt they allied with my husband at the time.

Another alarming tendency was for some parents to shift the blame onto the child, justifying their behaviour on the basis of control and discipline problems. One nine-year-old boy, for instance, showed physical marks of severe beating on more than one occasion. His mother explained:

> It all happened because I had to go out looking for him, then the school phoned about his rudeness. He came in two hours later covered in mud, when it was dark and he was whacked with a belt. The police said he was cruelly beaten, then said something about sexual abuse and there being no food in the house. Half of it was fabrication, fiction. And he was coached with his story by the older children. It is all right listening to children, but it is also good to make sure allegations are founded and beyond reasonable doubt.

By far the commonest scapegoats were social workers, blamed for unnecessarily escalating events or picking up on parents:

> They were against me from the day I had her. They said I wouldn't cope before she was even born and they had that idea all the way through.

> The social worker said she would make sure I would lose every kid, and I have. She was horrible.

Mr and Mrs Collins,* who had been involved in several sets of care proceedings over their son Sammi, conceded they had made a 'mistake' originally by leaving the children unattended while they went to a party, which brought them to the attention of the child protection system. They denied, however, responsibility for any of the dozens of non-accidental injuries which occurred subsequently, even though Sammi's allegation of ill-treatment was supported by his older sister. Instead they attributed them to the child's boisterousness,

* All names used throughout are fictitious.

the unsuitable environment and lack of supervision at nursery and Social Services' intervention to malice.

Exceptionally some parents did accept responsibility. One mother, for example, had lost all her children in turn as the result of her addiction to crack cocaine and at the time of proceedings was serving a prison sentence for offences of violence and theft. By the end of the proceedings she was ready to concede the Care Order and was only anxious that all three children should remain in contact, albeit in different adoptive homes. In interview she readily admitted her mistakes:

> The social workers wanted to help me, but when I was young, you don't want help. I do now, as I understand a bit more. I'm at the age where I know I don't know it all. You know you are doing something wrong, and the baby should be in good hands.

Other parents, however, even while more accepting of official concerns, remained angry and hurt about being dragged into the child protection process. This particularly applied to parents with psychiatric problems who, with improving health, clearer insights, support and sometimes the return of their children, were able to acknowledge the impact upon their children of the more acute stages of their illness. Despite a more convergent perspective on the nature of the problem they were therefore still critical of the way it had been dealt with.

Perspectives on local authority services

Not only was there little meeting of minds between Social Services and the majority of the parents in the study sample over the grounds for concern, parents were also generally extremely negative about the 'help' that had been made available to them in their often lengthy period of agency involvement. In 12 cases parents denied receiving any services at all, a claim which was easily disproved from the main study data. Those who acknowledged receiving some assistance generally did so begrudgingly and tended to under-report its extent, with few parents perceiving it to be substantial, sufficient, or appropriate. Even where a particular service was appreciated there were criticisms that it was inconsistent or withdrawn too soon.

Many parents were also ambivalent about accepting services, with 20% saying they would have preferred to 'paddle their own canoe' and others fearful of the consequences of not doing so:

> We rejected their help. We didn't want them interfering in our lives and blackmailing us when there was nothing wrong except that [older child] was in care.

> They never really helped me, just harassed me. I felt I was being harassed all the time. One stage down the nursery, I thought they were trying to help me, but I didn't know they were after my kids. I was exhausted and needed respite care for my children, but I refused it because I didn't think they were going to bring them back.

It would be dangerous, if easy, to dismiss this truly dismal picture. Pillorying Social Services as an uncaring, untrustworthy and predatory agency offers another useful device by which fragile and battered egos can protect themselves from unpalatable truths. Parents' accounts may often have been factually inaccurate or misleading, but what they conveyed most powerfully was a sense of desperate unmet need which it would be both inhumane and counter-productive to ignore.

Although, as we demonstrated earlier, parents were not generally prepared to accept the totality of official concerns, many of them did acknowledge that they had *some* family problems, which might conceivably have provided some common basis for action. Similarly many volunteered ideas for the forms of help they needed to address their difficulties.

The majority of these suggestions focused upon their own emotional needs arising from past or present life experiences. It will be recalled that a high proportion of these parents had themselves been abused as children and/or spent part of their childhood in public care, and several spoke of needing help to resolve their feelings about this. Some of the many mothers entangled within violent or abusive relationships felt that social workers had little grasp of the effect of domestic violence and rarely focused upon it as a problem. They would therefore have welcomed more support both emotionally and legally in securing their own protection.[6] As one mother put it:

> They just don't understand the situation when violence is present in the home. I needed much more support and help from them, not being ignored.

Overall there was resentment that Social Services' input, being focused upon deficits in the care of the children, was skewed, to the detriment of the parents who were trying to provide that care. A recurring theme was the need for a trusted befriender or confidante, with whom they could discuss their difficulties. It was notable that when, in a very few cases, this form of trust had been established by a particular worker, there was a shift towards a more positive perception of social work involvement.

The provision of help might be seen to be taking us back to the days of preventative family-orientated casework or alternatively forward to assistance to parents in their own right as troubled adults, alongside or perhaps independent from, the provision of child welfare services in the form of Section 17 legislation and general family support.[7] It is clear that this would be a desperately difficult task to attempt with parents whose low self-esteem and sense of failure may be expressed in alcohol or drug abuse and masked by hostility and aggression. It is skilled, time-consuming and demanding work which sits rather badly with the pressurised and increasingly managerial climate in which public agencies now find themselves functioning. Much will depend upon personal dynamics between worker and parent. It is also difficult to combine with a focus upon child protection without either endangering the child, as was all too evident in the case of Jasmine Beckford,[8] or neglecting the parent. It may be impossible for Social Services to achieve with parents who are bitter about their own childhood in care and who may feel they are being victimised for something which was beyond their control. In such cases the involvement of another agency may be the only hope of achieving a workable relationship.

The other strong positive theme to emerge was the desire for more attention to be paid to the practical realities of parents' lives. Inadequate, unsafe or squalid accommodation in particular was identified as a major stress factor adversely affecting the parents' ability to cope. It is unlikely that all the repeated injuries to Sammi Collins, for instance, could be directly attributed, at least to the extent that his parents claimed, to their poor housing. None the less, as the Guardian ad Litem pointed out in her report, both house and garden were undoubtedly dangerous. The task of supervising an energetic and rather reckless four-year-old in such a child-hostile environment would stretch the resources of any parent.[9] One does not need much empathy to imagine what it must have been like for Mrs Collins, still only 21, with two other under-fives and another expected and nervous that any bruise would be interpreted as non-accidental injury.

One of the services which did seem to be appreciated by parents was respite care. In the event, however, such positive experiences were largely eclipsed by the highly negative reactions of those parents whose children were accommodated at the point the local authority decided to take court action, an issue we considered worth exploring in more detail.

The use of accommodation

Data from our main sample of 83 cases suggest that accommodation is now a significant point of entry to the court process, 25% of proceedings being initiated in this way. Such cases were over-represented among the parents who agreed to be interviewed, ten cases (40%) involving accommodation. Eight of these concerned ethnic minority families.

Accommodation under the Children Act was conceived as part of the range of services available to help families in difficulty, the voluntary nature of the contract stressed by the removal of the requirement to give 28 days' notice of removal once the child had been in care for six months. Research by Packman and Hall[10] suggests that in most respects this is working well. It has become evident, however, that in at least some authorities accommodation is being used as part of the child protection strategy and offered to parents as an alternative to immediate court action. In our main sample just over half the cases involved this second use, what some practitioners term 'enforced' accommodation; in the interview sample this proportion reached 70%. This balance is reflected in the following highly critical accounts interviewees gave of their experiences of accommodation.

Parents feel coerced

Only three of the parents interviewed reported readily agreeing to accommodation in the first instance. The remainder told us they felt under pressure to comply, to be negotiating from a weak and powerless position which left them little option, to be 'blackmailed' and 'threatened' with court action if they did not agree. They complied as a means of getting Social Services 'off our backs' and avoiding being labelled 'uncooperative' rather than because accommodation provided a positive opportunity to work with the department. Many clearly maintained their own agendas on how far they were prepared to conform to the arrangements. The following extracts typify parents' feelings of powerlessness in their dealings with what they experienced as a coercive and all-powerful agency:

> I thought if I didn't agree they would get a Care Order on her. He said if I didn't sign they would go and get an EPO [Emergency Protection Order] on her and I would lose all my rights.

> I had no choice but to support it. I signed it to support my wife.

> They kept threatening me with an EPO if I didn't let them have their way with it. I didn't really agree to accommodation and reducing all contact to once a week.

> I signed it for a quiet life, to appear to be co-operating but I thought to myself, am I signing something I will regret, just to get them off my back?

Parents feel deceived

As this last comment indicates, a number of parents agreeing to accommodation did so with some foreboding, nagged by lingering doubts that they had taken the first step to losing their children. Most, however, appeared to believe, and all to hope, that the arrangement was short-term, giving respite from family stresses and allowing the children to return home once these were sorted out.[11]

> I had the belief that the children needed space with all that was happening. If I could have gone away, I could have had the children or moved out.

> I thought it was a cooling off period giving time and the children would be home.

Since in all the enforced cases children were accommodated after they had suffered significant harm it would seem that choosing the voluntary option does not require parents to face up to the real concerns about their care. Some appeared to have assumed that once they had agreed to accommodation, court proceedings were off the agenda. As the period of separation stretched from weeks into months, therefore,[12] parents came to feel disillusioned and – when court proceedings eventually ensued and most lost their children to substitute care – grossly deceived. Perceptions that they had been 'tricked' and manipulated as part of a long-term strategy to seize their children were reflected in such comments as:

> They just wanted my baby, that was it, I know it was like that.

> They treated me like a piece of dirt. They just wanted to get her away from us and never see her again.

Parents feel ill-informed

Parents persistently spoke of the need for more honesty, better information and good, independent advice, the lack of which hinders them from making genuine and carefully thought out choices and fuels their feelings of deception. As one parent put it:

> I never really understood you could fight it. They were only doing their job but it was not done properly because they didn't tell me my entitlements or my rights.

Most parents had not taken legal advice at the point accommodation was offered and subsequently regretted this. On the other hand those who had done so were of the opinion that they had been 'sold down the river' by solicitors who had, as they saw it, misled them, taken the line of least resistance and capitulated too easily to Social Services.

Parents feel confused about uncertain and changing goals

Given the apparent lack of agreement between agency and client about the purposes of accommodation it is scarcely surprising that parents reported feeling bewildered as to what they had been expected to do to satisfy the agency and thereby regain their children:

> The thing is you don't know what they want from you, what they are looking for, what they expect. Nobody tells you anything; they just carry on.

There were also complaints that targets had been unreasonable, but when parents inevitably defaulted they were again labelled as uncooperative or not really concerned about their children. When they did manage to improve their circumstances these were undervalued or deemed insufficient to meet the new goals which had by then been set.

Parents feel powerless

Throughout the process parents evidenced feelings of being powerless both to resist an all-powerful agency and to avert a train of events which in retrospect was seen as somehow inevitable, even pre-planned. Many described being in a 'no win' situation where the truth was distorted and used against them. As one told us:

> When we found out that because the children were in voluntary care we could have taken them home, Social Services changed and went for orders. In court they said we could have picked the children up any time, but we wouldn't, because we were trying to co-operate . . . The guardian said they were only accommodated and we could not have cared . . . Ironic isn't it?

Coerced, deceived, confused, ill-informed, manipulated, powerless. This is scarcely how accommodation was intended to make parents feel and anything further from partnership is difficult to imagine. Moreover, what these disaffected parents told us about their experiences of enforced accommodation was strongly confirmed by practitioners interviewed in the main study.

Together, these criticisms suggest that while accommodation *per se* may be functioning well, there needs to be some serious questioning about its use in difficult child protection cases and if the practice is to continue, more stringent safeguards against its abuse. Most important of all for parents would seem to be an independent source of information, advice and if necessary advocacy to ensure that there can be no possible justification in reality for parents continuing to regard accommodation as little more than a fraudulent plot.

Parental experiences of enforced accommodation provide perhaps the starkest contrast between ideals and reality. In essence, however, they also encapsulate much of what the whole group of parents were saying about their contact with Social Services prior to court proceedings.

The need for court action

As indicated earlier, the parents interviewed generally acknowledged that at the point when Social Services brought proceedings, they were experiencing problems, even if they tended to minimise the nature and severity of these. Most parents were also prepared to concede that Social Services were justified in having 'concerns', even though they regarded these as 'exaggerated' and Social Services to be 'picking on all our faults' or operating a gold standard of parenting which it was impossible to meet.

It was notable that where proceedings were precipitated by emergency action in the form of police protection or an Emergency Protection Order there was a much greater degree of congruence with the agency presentation and some recognition of the need for intervention (75%). These cases usually involved particular recent incidents or allegations of abuse and it is conjectured that sharper messages from child protection workers, such as the police or social workers, may have been more firmly expressed and targeted, with less room for ambiguities or misunderstandings and thus more readily absorbed. This recognition, however, did not extend to accepting court action, with only a quarter expressing satisfaction with the way things then developed.

In cases which did not begin with emergency protection, parents tended to be much more unconvinced that there were major reasons for concern. These cases tended to involve chronic neglect rather than abuse, or repeated minor injuries, failure to thrive or problems arising from generally chaotic lifestyles. Most also involved children who had been accommodated so that often some considerable time had elapsed since the parent had had care of the child.

Over 60% of parents admitted that they had received prior warning(s) from Social Services that court action was being considered. Given that the majority of parents failed to accept responsibility for their part in the abuse, the honest admission of a substantial number of warnings is fairly high. Parents, however, usually added the caveat that warnings had come too late or had been couched in such vague and ambiguous terms that they had failed to heed them. Our overall impression of the 'early warning system' is of an interactive game of brinkmanship with practitioners not giving sufficiently clear and authoritative messages and perhaps succumbing to a prevarication of numerous 'second chances', while parents disregarded or tested out the seriousness of the intent to take firmer action. Furthermore, because the perception was of Social Services 'crying wolf', when the axe eventually fell and parents found themselves in court, the enormity of the consequences and the power of the system impacted anew and they responded angrily or with acute distress.

Participation and partnership

Parental responsibility does not cease even when children are compulsorily removed into care and the ethos of the Children Act is that as far as possible, from the point of first contact, parents should be involved in decisions about their children.[13] As far as the parents in this study were concerned these high ideals are just so much pie in the sky. 'There should have been more negotiation before proceedings were started' was a common theme. As one father who described the intervention as 'heavy handed' put it:

> You need to work things more together with them. Social Services seem to do things first then question them and analyse the results afterwards.

In total, only 16% of parents felt that they had been involved in decision-making prior to proceedings, with the majority considering that Social Services had already prejudged their case and made their minds up about how they were to proceed. Consultation with parents was seen as merely paying lip-service to notions of participation, and attempts to involve them as patronising and condescending:

> How are you supposed to stop them? They just go ahead with their plans anyway, don't they? . . . They are too powerful.

> It was stupid because you don't get nowhere by it. It's just gabble gabble between themselves!

> They always have their own way, and don't listen half the time.

Parents whose care is on trial, many of whom subsequently lost their children, might of course be expected to have somewhat jaundiced views. It was striking, therefore, that even parents whose children had returned home had criticisms to make about what they perceived as the lack of consultation, inadequate information and intransigence of Social Services at this stage of the process. Moreover, similar complaints of marginalisation were made both by estranged fathers[14] and other relatives. Grandmothers appeared to feel particularly snubbed and acutely distressed by their lack of involvement:

> We had looked after the children and we were very concerned about them . . . They didn't even come and see us properly. They could have talked to me more about it; there was a lack of communication. They didn't give us information as to why they were doing things. I still feel Social Services have too much power and give them a bit of power they abuse it.

> They should have enquired about the blood relatives in the first place. It all took too much time and was damaging to the child.

Since the Children Act parents are much more likely to be involved in formal decision-making processes. Official guidance, for instance, states that parents should normally be invited to case conferences. All three authorities in the sample had policies encouraging parental attendance and 72% of the parents or relatives interviewed reported attending at least one case conference or formal meeting. It seems that the changes brought about by the Act in this respect command wide support among parents, given that all those who did attend considered it important to have done so, and those who were not invited were vociferous about being excluded. Indeed one mother with lengthy involvement with Social Services specifically commended the Children Act for enabling her to attend meetings which had previously been closed to her.

Only about half the parents, however, considered they had received adequate information or explanations about meetings which had enabled them to understand the significance of these events in the whole process. Such explanations came primarily from social workers (six cases); although solicitors were mentioned in three cases and the conference chair in another three. One professional couple, unfamiliar with Social Services procedures, said they had found the information sheet they were given informative and enlightening. None of the others seemed to have had the benefit of such written information though they told us it would have been welcome. It was again notable that parents reaching court via the EPO route were on the whole clearer about the purpose of meetings.

Official guidance also makes it clear that parents can be accompanied to meetings by a supporter of their own choice. Lawyers are specifically not excluded from attending though not in a representational capacity. However, more than half the parents who attended did so alone, either because they did not want anyone to witness their embarrassment and humiliation; because they had not been able to arrange a supporter on that day, or because they were unaware that they had a right to do so. Two parents reported not being allowed to bring their solicitor and one to bring a minister of religion who was also a personal friend.

Four parents (all in cases preceded by EPOs) were accompanied by their solicitors. All reported feeling more empowered, the mere attendance of the lawyer preventing Social Services 'getting away with anything' or 'trampling roughshod over our rights'. In contrast, the parents who attended alone seemed to be substantially more depressed about their level of participation and described meetings as 'daunting', 'feeling overwhelmed with long words', too inhibited to speak or misunderstood by practitioners. Parents who did venture to put forward their views, often felt 'foolish' or ignored:

> They don't listen.

> Your point of view never gets heard or understood.

Whether accompanied or not, most parents reported being intimidated by the size of the conference and many were disconcerted by the attendance of particular professionals such as a head teacher or agency representatives who had no personal knowledge of the family. The circumstances were often seen as stigmatising and individual professionals to be patronising, making parents feel 'like a lower person' or even 'like a murderer'. Parents cited instances in the meetings when they had not only been bewildered, angered or insulted by what was being said about them, but also felt harshly judged and unduly condemned. Some families complained of the cold and impersonal attitude of practitioners which left them feeling depersonalised by the experience. However, the most frequent complaint was simply of not being listened to adequately, which fuelled perceptions that everything had been prejudged in advance, in 'secret meetings' held before the main case conference. Exclusion from part of the conference served to increase these feelings of alienation and paranoia.

Overall 65% of parents or relatives felt their participation in Social Services meetings was generally poor and the impact of their attendance upon the decision-making process, insignificant. It was notable that the strongest adverse comments came from parents whose children had not been subject to emergency protection. Levels of satisfaction were also much higher and parents felt more able to make a fuller contribution to the discussion about the future of their children when parents had attended smaller and less formal meetings, sometimes conducted in an alternative venue such as a foster home, with more familiar key professionals.

Labelling and stigmatisation

A further barrier to partnership, as far as these families was concerned, was the fact that they felt prejudged and condemned:

> You were guilty before you were proved innocent. They just don't listen to you, you might as well have been sat watching the tele. They should stop prejudging you.

The majority of parents in the sample were struggling to bring up their children in adverse circumstances; many felt that as a result they had been unfairly labelled and stigmatised.[15] Parents suffering from diagnosed psychiatric illness were particularly distressed by the way they had been treated:

> They don't give you a chance. I mean if you are ill it is obvious you can't take care of yourself or the children and you can't guarantee you are not going to be ill can you? Social Services should be there to pick up the pieces, not cause a commotion. They treated me with great prejudice in my opinion.

> It does stigmatise you. That's how we feel.

> I am black British and a schizophrenic and they thought I was an idiot.

Other parents complained of stigmatisation because of drug or alcohol addiction, criminal activity or previous parenting difficulties:

> The social worker made me feel like a junkie and that there was no hope for me or the children. She wrote me off.

> Because I was in prison they didn't consider me. Just forget about him, he's a criminal.

> There should be less dwelling on past failures.

All this might be summed up in the plea:

> I wish they had treated me more as a person.

From a rather different angle a number of interviewees from ethnic minority groups commented that social workers sometimes failed to appreciate the extent to which the exposure of their parenting difficulties left them vulnerable to stigmatisation within their own communities.[16]

> They should try to understand the cultural levels of shame experienced about a court appearance which can be the last straw in damaging someone's life.

The baggage of negativity

In summary, then, the majority of parents interviewed held extremely negative perceptions about their contact with Social Services prior to court proceedings. Only 20% felt they had been treated with some consideration and fairness with 80% considering partnership had been poor. Social Services were widely considered to be biased, to have closed minds and to have narrowly focused upon the alleged abuse of the children to the exclusion of any consideration of the needs and circumstances of the adults. Parents felt impotent in the face of an all-powerful machine which had already made its judgement and found them wanting. Help which might have been offered in the past was undervalued or even, by some, seen in the context of a plot to snatch the children away. Those who at one time might have trusted their social worker now felt disillusioned, deceived and betrayed.

At the point of entering the court process, most of these parents were therefore carrying a considerable baggage of negativity having undergone a process which had been experienced as clinical, heartless, impersonal and coercive, about which they had inadequate information and in which they felt they had little power. They were now to be thrust into a legal process which is not conspicuous for its user-friendliness. Understandably most felt uncertain, fearful and insecure. It is to their experiences within that process that we now turn.

NOTES

[1] Section 31 (2).

[2] Hunt J; Macleod A (1999): *The Last Resort: Child Protection, the Courts and the 1989 Children Act*. The Stationery Office.

[3] Matza D; Sykes G (1957): 'Techniques of neutralisation: a theory of delinquency'. *American Sociological Review*, 22, pp 664–70.

[4] Abel GG; Becker JV; Mittleman M (1987): 'Self-reported sex crimes of non-incarcerated paraphiliacs'. *Journal of Interpersonal Violence*, Vol 2, pp 3–25. Finkelhor D (ed) (1986): 'Abusers: special topics' in Finkelhor D and Baron L: *A Source Book on Child Sexual Abuse – New Theory and Research*. Sage, Beverley Hills.

[5] Mechanic D (1978): *Medical Sociology*. (2nd edition). Free Press, New York.

[6] Stanko E (1988): 'Fear of crime and the myth of the safe home' in Borad M; Yuo K: *Feminist Perspectives on Wife Abuse*. Sage, London.

[7] Section 17 of the Children Act 1989. See also Aldgate J; Tunstill J (1998): *Children in Need*. Research report to Department of Health.

[8] London Borough of Brent (1995): *A Child in Trust: Report of the Panel of Inquiry Investigating the Circumstances Surrounding the Death of Jasmine Beckford*. Kingswood Press.

[9] Rutter M; Quinton D; Liddle C (1983): 'Parenting in two generations: looking backwards and looking forwards' in Madge N: *Families at Risk*. London, DHSS.

[10] Packman J; Hall C (1998): *From Care to Accommodation*. The Stationery Office.

[11] Packman J; Hall C (1998): *op. cit.* Aldgate J (1993): 'Respite care for children: an old remedy in a new package' in Marsh P and Triseliotis J (eds): *Prevention and Reunification in Child Care*. Batsford.

[12] In the sample overall the average length of time in accommodation was 34 weeks.

[13] Social Services Inspectorate (1995): *The Challenge of Partnership in Child Protection*.

[14] Moss P (ed) (1995): *Father Figures: Fathers in the Families of the 1990s*. HMSO.

[15] Cuff EC; Payne GCF (1962): 'Paranoia and the dynamics of exclusion in Perspectives in Sociology'. *Sociometry*, Vol 25.

[16] Cheetlam J (ed) (1982): *Social Work and Ethnicity*. NISS Library no 43. Allen & Unwin.

4 *The court forum*

Preparation for court

> I thought it was going to be like *LA Law*.

> I thought there was going to be a judge and jury.

> I didn't realise the hearing would be private.

As these quotations suggest, the majority of the parents interviewed (21 cases) considered themselves to have been ill-prepared for proceedings. For some parents it was their first encounter with the court system, whilst others could only draw on their experiences with the adult criminal or civil courts, or perhaps with the juvenile court. A few had had experience of care or wardship proceedings but of course not under the Children Act.

This is not to say that parents had not received any preparation; on the contrary only three said they were in this position. Fourteen remembered being given verbal information from their solicitors, five from social workers and two from the Guardian ad Litem. However it seems this largely involved stating who would be attending court and while parents found this helpful it had not prepared them for the layout of the courtroom, the adversarial system or the legal language in which the cases would be conducted.

It is possible, of course, that, as experience of medical consultations demonstrates, parents were so distressed that they were unable to take in everything they were told or that it was considered inappropriate at this point to go over it. As one couple told us:

> We were shocked and confused and you don't retain everything.

Verbal information, however, was only rarely supplemented by written material, with only five parents reporting receiving information from Social Services and one parent from both a solicitor and a guardian. Moreover, nobody considered that what they had received was either very pertinent nor helpful, tending to relate to the Children Act in broad terms rather than specifically focusing upon the court process.

Thus a theme common to almost all our interviews, typified in the quotations which follow, was a plea for more and better targeted information:

> I needed more help. If I had had someone who had explained to me what was going on it would have been easier for me.

> I needed more help and explanation with what was going on and understanding things.

> More advice about the court proceedings, more explanations and help from the social workers, in fact information as well as who to approach.

> I needed more advice about the Children Act, child protection and the courts.

> I needed more help knowing about the system.

Many interviewees also volunteered concrete suggestions as to how parents who found themselves in court in future might be better prepared. Examples included: a booklet written in uncomplicated language, which provided specific and basic information about how hearings are conducted and 'what our rights are'; 'Visiting the courtroom and meeting the judge'; or (perhaps more practically) 'the chance to view some kind of training video', the chance to practise speaking in public.

These ideas do not seem outrageous. It is now, belatedly, accepted that children need familiarisation with the court system before they appear as witnesses[1] – and the needs of litigants in civil proceedings to have access to good information is highlighted in the *Woolf Report*.[2] Clearly, parents in care proceedings also have unmet needs and the production of a booklet and a video at least would seem to be ideas worth pursuing. The information booths referred to in the *Woolf Report* were not among the parents' suggestions, though they might have a place. Generally, though, we would anticipate parents being too 'keyed up' when they attend court to make effective use of such a facility and too fearful to go there unaccompanied beforehand. It would be quite different of course, if parents could be taken to the court in advance by someone who was also available to answer their questions and deal with their anxieties, another suggestion made by some parents.

Failing this the production of a booklet and/or video would seem to be a realistic proposition. Both could be made available through Social Services departments, solicitors' offices or Citizens' Advice Bureaux while booklets could additionally be sent out by the court with the notice of the first hearing. Such measures would help to prevent ignorance and fantasies unnecessarily compounding the natural apprehension parents feel when entering a process with such potentially dire consequences.

Waiting at court

Parents were unanimous (and vociferous) in reporting high levels of anxiety and distress as they waited to go into court for the first time, describing the experience as 'frightening' (7), 'nerve-racking' (6), 'terrible', 'horrible', or 'awful' (4) and reactions such as 'smoking my head off', 'crying', 'swearing a lot', 'stomach going over' and even 'being sick'.

These natural and perhaps inevitable feelings of apprehension were exacerbated by having to wait in a public arena, the most common complaint being lack of privacy: 'noisy and lots of people around', 'too busy'. As a result parents, who may already have felt subject to a degree of community disapproval by virtue of having their children removed, felt 'stared at':

> People always around me. I felt they were looking at me and wondering.

While five parents reported being able to go into side-rooms, most felt there was nowhere to go to escape an exposure they felt was 'degrading', 'embarrassing' or 'made me feel like a criminal'. If they wanted to talk some said they 'had to whisper . . . in case we were overheard'.

Imagine then feeling like this *and* having to wait for your case to be called for a lengthy and indeterminate period. Only seven parents reported going into court more or less immediately and four within an hour; the remainder recalled much longer periods than this. Lest this should be attributed to the differential flow of time according to what is happening, a phenomenon we have all experienced, we should point out that our court observation data broadly confirm these recollections.[3]

Practitioners, of course, are accustomed to hearings not starting on time; indeed they seem to operate on the basis that they will not and often use the time productively to negotiate with the other parties. Parents, however, found the 'hanging around' irritating 'because you couldn't go anywhere in case you were called'. One parent said:

> They muck you around. You should be given a time and they should stick to it.

In spite of their anxiety parents were not oblivious to their surroundings and as in previous research[4] court waiting areas attracted many adverse comments with 15 sets of parents complaining of poor facilities and premises which they described as: 'cold and dreary, made me feel worse', 'not that nice', 'not that clean' or even 'squalid'. Parents' suggestions for improvements were practical, straightforward and relatively cheap: comfortable seating, a snack bar or at least a drinks machine and smoking areas were high on the list for change and where such facilities existed they were appreciated. They do not seem unreasonable, especially bearing in mind the trend to introduce these types of facilities in hospitals where patients or visitors may experience comparable levels of anxiety.

Such minor innovations of comfort might mitigate in some measure the trauma of waiting, while helping parents to feel treated with some humanity and dignity and less on trial. As one mother urged:

> It would help to treat people like human beings and not like they are dirt all the time.

Difficulties in attending court

Such experiences are all the more irritating, even distressing, when a parent has made a great effort to be there. Half the parents interviewed recalled having difficulties attending court. Two mothers, one partially sighted and one subject to anxiety states and phobias, found having to go a considerable distance on public transport particularly nail-biting, while the unreliability and expense was a handicap for many and the cost of taxi services prohibitive for those on low incomes. Lifts to court, usually by the solicitor or social worker, were therefore very much appreciated.

Most of the sample families, it will be recalled, were dependent upon state benefits. However, working parents also experienced difficulties. One couple found the prospect of having to divulge details of their personal lives in order to get time off particularly shaming, while for all those in employment the loss of working time and subsequent stoppage of earnings was a major anxiety. Three fathers working night shifts found it hard to make hearings scheduled early in the morning and, one imagines, hard to stay awake during them.

Somewhat surprisingly, only one parent reported child care difficulties; although one of the courts had crèche facilities it seems that on the whole parents' informal networks were called upon to help. This could mean, however, that they were not available to offer support to the parents themselves by accompanying them to court.

Isolation, exclusion and confusion

The isolation of parents both in and outside court is often heart-rending. Fourteen parents told us they would have liked someone with them in court. It is exceptional, however, for a friend or supporter to be allowed into the courtroom itself while relatives are usually only there because they have a direct interest in proceedings which may be at odds with the parents'. Sometimes, of course, a parent may be trying to prevent knowledge of their situation becoming known, telling us 'I was ashamed'; 'I didn't want my family or friends to know'; and 'I wanted to keep it quiet from my Mum'. Others were estranged from their families, perceived them as unhelpful, or saddest of all, told us 'I haven't got no friends'.

Parental isolation can also be highlighted by the clubby atmosphere of some court waiting areas. The camaraderie which understandably develops among professionals who work together frequently – which can indeed work to the benefit of the client – looks rather different to a parent unfamiliar with the culture. Negotiation between representatives in the absence of the client is also part of the legal culture which professionals accept, may indeed take for granted. For parents, however, such exclusion adds to their sense of isolation, even perhaps paranoia, as they sat 'huddled together' while all the professionals were either 'behind closed doors', whispered around them 'wheeling and dealing' or spoke to each other in language which was beyond parental comprehension.

Additional confusion was introduced into the process when the venue for hearings did not remain the same throughout. Only five cases were heard throughout in the same building in which they started but almost half the remaining parents 'didn't have a clue' why there had been a change. One mother said she had gone to the wrong court on a number of occasions and others said this sort of error had caused them to be late.

As time went on the experience of going to court became less stressful for nine of the parents interviewed, as the result, they told us, of knowing what to expect and receiving better support from their solicitors. However, even those parents who hoped things might be going their way remained anxious and insecure about the final outcome so that for the majority their anxiety level remained high, indeed even heightened as the final hearing grew closer and 'the pressure began to build up'.

Thus each time they came to court parents had to 'psych themselves up' for an experience they knew would be extremely upsetting: 'traumatic throughout'; 'awful seeing everyone all the time'; 'trying, time-consuming and distressing'; 'I thought I would get my child back every time'; 'we didn't know what they were going to do next'. It is therefore much to their credit that so many persevered. Seventeen of the parents interviewed said they had attended all the hearings on their case and most of the others had missed only occasional hearings, usually for what appeared to be legitimate reasons. Again parents did not seem to have been exaggerating their attendance, since this corresponds with the rates noted in our main study.

Such high attendance reflects the hopes parents had invested in the court process. It was apparent that though these parents might be considered abusive or neglectful in the eyes of society, their children still meant a great deal to them and their potential loss from the family was something most were determined to fight in the only forum they saw left to them. Thus they saw the court as the final arbiter and court proceedings as the way in which they could clear their names. Good attendance was part and parcel of that scenario. As one interviewee stated:

> I will move myself for the court, but not for Social Services.

In court

Feeling ill-prepared and ill at ease outside the courtroom, their uncomfortable experience was perpetuated for parents in the courtroom itself. The theme of greater participation and equal status within a process in which they ought to be major players, which emerged in parents' reflections on their prior encounters with Social Services, was voiced just as vehemently in relation to their courtroom appearance.

Seating arrangements

At the most basic level, their physical position in court gave out some powerful messages to parents about the degree of respect in which they were held, the extent to which they were expected to participate and the level of support which would be forthcoming.

Some parents found themselves sitting behind their lawyers or, even worse, confined to the back of the room where, they felt, they 'might as well not have been there'. Only one young mother, who remained terrified by a particular judge throughout proceedings, was intensely relieved to be able to hide away at the back of the courtroom 'so I couldn't be seen by him'. Five of these parents were not only symbolically, but practically, excluded from the process because they were unable to hear particularly soft spoken participants from their position at the back of the courtroom, an experience to which the researchers, also struggling to hear what was going on, can attest. Consequently several interviewees, including a grandmother who was hard of hearing anyway, urged the use of microphones. This is a problem reported on in previous court-based projects.[5]

Neither, however, were arrangements ideal for the small number of parents placed right in the front of the court facing the Bench, who found this proximity and exposure made them feel uneasy or embarrassed:

> I felt the magistrate was watching me thinking: 'How can a mother let that happen?'

Parents were more satisfied when they sat towards the front of the courtroom and, crucially, next to their own lawyers, to whom they could give immediate instructions or whisper comments. The best arrangement of all, however, was to be placed around a table, ideally next to their legal representatives or other supportive practitioners:

> I prefer a round table, because otherwise people are staring at you at the front and there are people behind you talking about you over your head.

Although we understand that many Family Proceedings Courts have now adopted this model, there were only five cases in the sample where parents reported experiencing it.

Giving evidence

If, as is clear, parents felt exposed and vulnerable when they were positioned right at the front of the court, not surprisingly they felt even more intimidated when they went into the witness box 'with all those faces looking at you'.

More than half of our interviewees, however, were not given even this option to speak in the court, although many claimed they would at least liked to have been asked. Their comments suggest that this opportunity would have given them a feeling of equal status and validity in the proceedings, rather than subsequently feeling ignored, depersonalised, inconsequential and insulted.

> I wasn't even asked one question; I think I might as well have been a dummy in the court.

> I mean they treated me like a schoolgirl with no sense and didn't appreciate
> I am no rag doll but a 30-year-old woman.

Clearly this is a matter which needs to be approached carefully. Few of the parents who did give evidence felt they had acquitted themselves well, some even bungling their performance as the result of 'nerves', their state of mind at the time, or simply inexperience in speaking out in a public and intimidating forum. Even a father with acting experience, however, was said by his wife to have made a 'wobbly' start until he 'warmed up' in the witness box. He confirmed this, telling us:

> I got very confused in court about what I was saying and I felt more like
> a criminal.

Another common problem was feeling rushed, with several parents complaining they had been given insufficient time to complete what they wanted to say:

> There were always too many other speakers.

> The hearing was too quick. It is always like that in court. You are only allowed
> to say it briefly and they don't let you explain.

> There was no time to say how you felt before they would go on to something
> else when you were giving your answers.

Giving formal evidence, it would seem, demands precision skills which parents do not possess. The pressure experienced, combined with the awesome occasion, left even normally articulate parents feeling they had failed to do themselves justice. Even so, none of the parents ultimately regretted attempting to put their point of view. This suggests that with greater preparation and a degree of sensitivity, encouragement and forbearance on the part of practitioners and the judiciary, parents might do a better job with consequent beneficial effects upon their sense of justice.

It is rare, of course, for witnesses giving evidence in chief not to be cross-examined and this was unequivocally one of the most difficult and disliked aspects of the process. There was a plethora of complaints, including: lack of comprehension of questions couched in legal language; irrelevant questions; questions 'coming out of the blue'; lack of time to complete answers; and feeling humiliated, deceived or personally attacked or above all confused. These comments are typical:

> They repeated the same questions over and over again and didn't want to take my first answer.

> It wasn't in my own words or in my way. I would have understood otherwise.

> The local authority solicitor put across questions in such a way it made me feel small and he tried to double-cross me with questions that I didn't understand.

> The questions required a study of the Queen's English.

Many of the adverse comments about cross-examination, as can be seen, focused upon the need to simplify language and make it comprehensible to the man in the street. It cannot be assumed that parents will ask if they fail to understand, preferring to settle for saving face while feeling privately foolish, judging from the comment of one highly intimidated mother who stated:

> You couldn't ask them to repeat things because the judge would have sent me out of the room.

Such a barrage of criticism challenges the appropriateness of the conventional adversarial approach in such sensitive child care matters where parents are after all not in the dock on a criminal charge, but involved in a civil action about the future well-being of their children. Not only are vulnerable parents ill-prepared for this assault on their family life and personal integrity, but welfare agencies subsequently have to pick up the pieces of shattered lives when these traumatic events have ended, and are still obliged to work in partnership with angry, alienated and wounded parents.

Bringing evidence

If parents generally felt that their own evidence had not assisted their case very much, nor did they get much help from the evidence of others. Fewer than half (10) had their own expert witnesses, indeed many were unaware that this was even a possibility. While parents were grateful when professionals said positive things about them, in practice this was perceived to be fairly rare.

Moreover many parents felt evidence derived from more familiar figures in their daily lives, such as close friends or relatives, would have been more appropriate and would have helped them to counter the local authority stance. They expressed much resentment that witnesses were generally appearing in a professional capacity rather than by virtue of having been socially intimate or having regularly observed their family life. Parents told us that in many instances the latter had been excluded from the proceedings, leaving a sense of injustice that the court was only getting a fragmented view of their lives which emphasised their personal faults and parenting failures. Such evidence as was permitted from witnesses who were more acceptable to parents was perceived as being given insufficient weight and ineffective in changing the outcome. Indeed, as others on the research team observed, sometimes such evidence, quite inadvertently, seemed to be the final nail in the coffin. This is presumably one of the many factors that solicitors seeking to act on their client's instructions while also promoting their best interests, constantly have to juggle.

Challenging the evidence

Under the Children Act all parties are required to disclose in advance the substance of any evidence upon which they intend to rely.[6] This is a significant advance on pre-Act care proceedings when parents' lawyers often complained of being impeded in their case preparation because they were unaware of what the parents were accused. Sometimes they deliberately chose to contest the first interim order in an effort to size up the opposition. Most evidence was oral – written evidence usually consisting only of reports submitted for the final hearing from the social worker and the Guardian ad Litem. Parents and their representatives might not be informed of the contents of those reports until the hearing was imminent, sometimes indeed not until the day of the hearing.[7]

Those manifest injustices have, fortunately, passed with the Act. The local authority is required to outline its case in the initial application and to amplify this in a supporting statement. This is typically updated by supplementary statements from the social worker and other professionals which all have to be copied to the parents' representatives in advance. Half the parents interviewed considered they had received statements or reports in sufficient time. Nonetheless it seems some vestiges of pre-Act problems remain, with eight parents recalling receiving reports just prior to a hearing and having to do a hasty scan of the alleged facts, snatching a consultation with their solicitor as they entered the courtroom. It was, unfortunately, unclear whether parents were mostly referring to interim hearings, where the research team observed that statements were frequently exchanged during the waiting period, or final hearings, where this was unusual. Nor was it possible to determine why this had happened, in particular whether it was due to tardiness on the part of the other parties or poor communication between a parent and his/her lawyer.

Parents generally reported getting the gist of what was contained in the written evidence, though again making a plea that language could be purged of jargon and simplified, complaining of 'long words and not using basic English'. When we asked about the content of the evidence, however, and whether it was perceived to be fair and accurate, we hit a minefield of negative and angry comments about Social Services, even amongst parents who were subsequently working well with them. Accusations of fabrications, exaggerations and distortions ranged from inaccuracies in dates and names, to blaming the wrong partner for the abuse or labelling the parent as the result of past errors:

> There were a hell of a load of things they had made up; a load of lies, it makes you laugh reading it.

> If they get something on you, they enlarge it so much and they miss so much out.

In most cases it was difficult to obtain any specific details to back up parental claims. Nevertheless, these responses emphasise the need for practitioners to take great care to be accurate in their statements as it would seem not all parental perceptions are without foundation. Moreover parents may focus upon relatively minor errors of fact, compounding or justifying their perceptions that a false picture has been presented.

How information is obtained and presented can also be offensive. One set of parents objected not only to the 'little potted statements about what we were like' but the fact that the social worker had acquired much of her information by phoning around the extended family without the parents' permission or prior knowledge.

For the first time in care proceedings parents now have a right to challenge these perceived inaccuracies and distortions by submitting their own statements. This was generally welcomed. Indeed whilst most parents had help from their solicitors in setting out what they wanted to say, two parents told us they actually went as far as writing their statements themselves, so determined were they to challenge the case against them and dispute the alleged facts. There was a widespread perception, however, that compared with those of professionals, their statements counted for little. One mother who had spent much time on her initial statements told us of her disillusionment:

> It annoyed me: what is the point of spending all that time and using your brain, when they don't want to know.

When parents were asked about the statements made about them verbally in court and whether these were perceived to be honest or fair, the same accusations resurfaced, with only two parents perceiving Social Services' evidence to have been fair. Individual social workers came in for a barrage of invective, being variously accused of lying, distorting facts, judging things out of context, dragging up outdated or irrelevant information or making gross mistakes in their presentation of the evidence. Parents felt once again the focus was highly selective, social workers having 'only kept notes on the bad bits'. One parent, conversant with the legal concept of significant harm, felt the evidence given by Social Services against them was too hypothetical, not grounded in reality and that their assessment of risk to the case children consisted repeatedly of 'what if?' This father spoke for many when he told us:

> We didn't have a chance to challenge things; a phrase or sentence would place things out of context.

Despite their anger at what was being said about them many parents reported feeling so beaten down and disempowered by this stage in the proceedings that they were unable to challenge errors in open court, waiting instead until after the hearing to inform their solicitor of their disagreement with the evidence. In at least eight cases parents said there were things they had not mentioned at all:

> Because what was the point as it was all sewn up.

However, or whatever they presented, the theme seemed to be: parents remained effectively powerless against the system. Even the two parents who did manage to challenge statements in open court still felt written off. As one mother stated:

> Because alcoholics are liars and deniers and who is going to believe them?

She continued by describing her feelings of despondency, graphically reporting she could not stop crying for days after her court experience:

> You could feel yourself going down, going under, like you are accused.

Improving the process

Is it possible to make an experience which is inherently traumatic any better for parents? A minority of parents thought this was impossible. Earlier in this chapter we reported parents' ideas on preparation for court and improvements to court waiting areas. Most parents were equally forthcoming in their ideas for improving the court process, some of which have been signalled in previous sections, such as the opportunity to present personal witnesses in court and more sensitive seating arrangements.

Parents would also like courts to function more efficiently. Lengthy and unpredictable waiting times were interpreted by parents not only as a sign of discourtesy to them but as a measure of the general inefficiency of the court system. They saw evidence of this in hearings which stopped and started, in the number of hearings which appeared to be necessary, in the amount of time spent waiting around while judges or magistrates read the papers or in familiarising a new judge with the case because he had not done his homework in advance.

Two over-arching themes, however, should be highlighted. First, the need for a more appropriate forum. Whether as a result of the formality of the setting and the procedures, the adversarial process or the convoluted language, parents experienced proceedings as intimidating, disabling and depersonalising. What they would like to see is a more informal setting in which they could take part in a comprehensible discussion of their circumstances and speak directly to those who will be taking the decisions:

> It would be helpful if magistrates talked to the parents and had direct discussion.

> Why can't magistrates take parents to one side and talk to them? They should all be more approachable.

> It's called the Family Court but they don't involve the family.

> It should be more like a family meeting than a court.

What the parents in this sample were clearly asking for is very akin to the model of participative justice suggested by Murch many years ago.[8] The authors' knowledge, albeit limited, of other family justice systems also suggests that the English care courts are rather more formalised, professionalised and rule-bound than is generally the case in other jurisdictions, even those not so far away.[9] The time perhaps has now come to look more seriously at other models, to develop a form of family justice which accords more closely not only with the expressed needs of families but with the values of partnership and participation which so strongly imbue the Children Act.

The second recurring theme, mentioned in some form or other by most parents, was their need for an independent supporter throughout proceedings. Reiterating their own ignorance of the process with such comments as:

> My little girl had never been in care before and I didn't have a clue what was going on.

> I knew nothing about the system and didn't understand it.

they told us:

> You need someone for yourself, an adult worker.

> Someone independent with authority that understands the procedures.

> Someone to explain all the papers.

> Someone to talk to.

> Someone to be a counsellor.

> Someone independent who will help you examine ways of rehabilitating the children.

Clearly at the moment this 'someone' does not generally exist. Parents' feelings towards social workers will usually be at best ambivalent if not downright hostile and suspicious; the guardian's responsibility is to the child whose interests may conflict with the parents. A few parents were able to turn to voluntary organisations like Barnardos, Family Service Units or the National Society for the Prevention of Cruelty to Children (NSPCC) and others to foster parents but again these will have a primary duty to the child. None of the families in the sample mentioned the existence of organisations such as the Family Rights Group or the self-help groups which exist in some areas. Even solicitors, who, as we shall see in the next chapter, are seen as both partisan and supportive, appear not to be meeting the need. Social workers and/or counsellors working with solicitors might be one way forward and we are aware that a few specialist family law firms do have this facility. Unfortunately none of the families in this survey had access to this kind of support so although in principle this would seem a promising way forward we are unable to comment on whether in reality it fills the gap which is so clearly there at the moment.

In the next chapter we examine parents' opinions about some of the key practitioners they encountered during their passage through the legal process.

NOTES

[1] Spencer JR; Flin RH (1993): *The Evidence of Children: the Law and the Psychology*. (2nd edition). Blackstone Press.

[2] Woolf LF (1995): *Access to Justice: Interim Report to the Lord Chancellor on the Civil Justice System in England and Wales*.

[3] Hunt J; Macleod A (1999): *The Last Resort: Child Protection, the Courts and the 1989 Children Act*. The Stationery Office.

[4] Hilgendorf L (1980): *Social Workers and Solicitors in Child Care Cases*. Tavistock Institute of Human Relations. Murch M; Hunt J; Macleod A (1990): *Representation of the Child in the Civil Courts: Summary and Recommendations to the Department of Health*. Socio-Legal Centre for Family Studies, University of Bristol.

[5] Murch M; Borkowski M; Copner C; Griew K (1987): *The Overlapping Jurisdiction of Magistrates' Courts and County Courts*. Socio-Legal Centre for Family Studies, University of Bristol.

[6] *Family Proceedings Court Rules 1991* r17 (1) and *Family Proceedings Rules 1991* r4 (17) (1).

[7] Murch; Hunt; Macleod (1990): *op. cit.*

[8] Murch M (1980): *Justice and Welfare in Divorce*. Sweet and Maxwell.

[9] For example, the Scottish hearing system or the French *Juge des enfants*. See Hetherington R (1994): 'Trans-Manche partnerships'. *BAAF Quarterly Review*, Vol 18, no 3.

5 *Practitioners in the legal process*

It will already be abundantly evident that in acting as a conduit for parental perceptions we have, unavoidably, conveyed some harsh messages about social work intervention. Even with good intentions and individual examples of good practice, social service departments, as the agents of statutory intervention, are the obvious scapegoats for parental anger. What about the other practitioners in the frame: lawyers, Guardians ad Litem and the judiciary?

Solicitors acting for parents

All the parents we interviewed had been legally represented and legally aided, even though some sought legal advice only after Social Services had advised them to do so. Most saw legal representation as crucial in defending themselves against the onslaught on their personal integrity, without which they would stand no chance of success. This reflects their lack of confidence in being able to function in an adversarial legal system as well as perhaps an assumption that 'you can't go to court without a solicitor to defend yourself'. There were only two cases where dissatisfied parents said that, if faced with similar circumstances again, they would prefer to represent themselves.

It was notable that only eight of the parents interviewed were represented by solicitors with specific child care or family law expertise. This reflects the way most parents (18) had sought legal advice from solicitors who were recommended by family or friends or who had acted for them in the past in criminal or divorce proceedings. The remaining families had taken 'pot luck'.

From their different vantage point the research team on the main study have expressed a certain amount of disquiet about the quality of parental representation and argued that action needs to be taken to address this. Undoubtedly the parents we interviewed would have appreciated being able to make an informed choice. It has to be said, however, that only one parent said she regretted her choice on these grounds saying:

> If I had used a child care specialist from the beginning the case would have been very different and there would have been a different outlook now, but it's too late.

Indeed only five cases produced any major negative criticism of the solicitor's professionalism. These parents variously alleged incompetence and laziness, lack of commitment, contact or communication or an impersonal and brusque manner. For example:

> He was lazy. He never sat down and explained nothing. He never came and saw me in prison. I wouldn't recommend him to other parents, they would be coming back to get me!

> I'd never recommend him again; he caved in a bit and I felt he could have been more committed.

> It seemed tedious for them, just a job.

One mother, describing her solicitor as 'defeatist' recalled receiving, and resisting, this blunt advice:

> I said I wanted to fight it and she said don't be stupid, you will never win. No, do it on your own next time.

Finally, one set of parents reported seeing their solicitor doing his financial accounts during the course of one hearing. They were, needless to say, incensed!

In general, however, parents reported a high level of satisfaction with the support they had received from their solicitors, the challenge they put up in court and the overall standard of service including advice, explanations, preparation of the case, understanding and contact. This complimentary perception does not seem to have been affected by the outcome since in reality, rather more parents 'lost' their cases than won them.

Otherwise satisfied parents were nonetheless critical about the lack of continuity in their representation at hearings with almost half experiencing some change. For some parents this was a source of confusion and insecurity – an indication that they could not expect a totally reliable service; for others an indication of lack of personal interest and commitment.

What, in the eyes of parents, makes a good solicitor? Undoubtedly winning a case helps – or at least being partisan and committed enough to put up a good fight on their behalf and show a personal interest in them and their children. Being caring and understanding and developing a rapport with the client was particularly valued, and contrasted with what might be perceived as the judgemental attitudes of some other professionals. Being prepared to listen, an old chestnut perhaps, was nonetheless vital: parents valued the opportunity to unload some of their burden on to someone else's shoulders. Feeling 'believed' was also a vital ingredient in helping parents cope with the emotional crisis submerging them.

Parents valued solicitors who involved them in discussions, negotiations and decision-making, whether about court orders or other applications, expert evidence or contact arrangements. Those who were able to advise, inform and explain in simple, direct and honest language were highly rated:

> His attitude was great and straight to the point, not using technical jargon. Brilliant, we have already recommended him.

Again these evaluations contrast favourably with parental perceptions of social work ambiguity, lack of clarity and deviousness.

At the risk of being accused of gender bias there did seem to be some preference for female solicitors (indeed also for female barristers and judges) reflected in the comments of both men and women. The explanation for this may be linked to traditional gender stereotyping of women as sensitive and caring and more in touch with child care matters – or it may be that women lawyers are more comfortable than their male colleagues with the less explicit supportive rather than the purely representational aspects of the role.

Barristers

In nearly half our cases (12) parents were also represented, at least on occasion, by barristers. In general their involvement was perceived as a major asset, giving parents confidence that they had armed themselves more effectively for the courtroom contest: 'We thought we'd give the case our best go'. In reality, however, we found that parents with barristers were more likely to lose than those who had only a solicitor, though one assumes this is a reflection of the difficulty of the case rather than respective competencies.

There were only two cases where parents were disappointed with the service they had received, maintaining they would not recommend others to use counsel because of their barrister's perceived lack of knowledge or unfamiliarity with the details of their case. One mother was blunt about her disillusionment:

> She was an idiot. She didn't seem to know the case against me. They are all useless. I've got a low opinion of all of them.

Most parents were ecstatic, describing their counsel as 'very good', 'brilliant' even 'fantastic'. While a confident court performance was clearly relevant to this appraisal, personal characteristics of warmth, understanding and humour were also much appreciated:

> She had the personality and style to go down well in court.

> She was very nice; she had a good sense of humour. I could talk to her.

In one case a mother who was disappointed with her solicitor's efforts in court, took the view that:

> It is advisable to have a barrister. Others may have to do the job properly for you if your own solicitor doesn't stick up for you.

Thus the introduction of a higher status lawyer gave parents a greater sense of empowerment in court, helping them to perceive the contest as fairer, even if this did not enable them to win their case.

Children's solicitors

Parents are surrounded by lawyers in the court setting and as part of examining their overall comprehension of the system we sought to explore how far they had been able to distinguish the varying roles. Perhaps surprisingly, the majority of parents (20) were aware that children had their own representative, though only about half appreciated the rationale. Where children were young some parents could not see the justification for a solicitor because, as one parent put it:

> They say they are putting forward the child's point of view but how is she supposed to have one when she is only ten months old.

Another questioned the whole principle of separate representation on the grounds that:

> There should be one solicitor for the family, unless the child is bringing the family to court. They should look at the best interests of the family as a whole. Children have rights but sometimes a mother knows what's best for you more than anyone.

Slightly more parents felt that there was a need for legal representation to defend the child's rights, protect their best interests and generally 'be on their side':

> You need one for the child's rights and to represent children's needs and wishes.

If one were to be optimistic this might indicate that the philosophy as well as the terminology of the Children Act is percolating through to parents, even those who have been accused of neglecting or abusing their children.

Contact with the child's solicitor was valued though it happened rarely, a fact of which several parents were critical. While this may indicate that some solicitors are discourteous it also suggests that parents do not appreciate the rules of the game. Indeed there was much confusion about the respective roles of the Guardian ad Litem and the child's solicitor. Criticism, for instance, that the child's solicitor 'only listens to what the guardian tells them' suggests the duty of the child's solicitor to take instructions from the guardian (other than in certain limited circumstances) had not been adequately explained. If so one could speculate that this might compound parents' feelings that the scales are weighted against them particularly if they perceive the guardian as being unduly influenced by the local authority.

The Guardian ad Litem

This, unfortunately, was the case as far as 11 of our families were concerned. Indeed, it was the single most important criticism to emerge, reflecting a substantial credibility gap expressed as lingering suspicion or deep conviction that guardians colluded with or were heavily influenced by what Social Services said. For instance:

> I didn't believe she was independent. She was on their side.

> He was seeing a lot of Social Services and I felt he was getting their side of the story all the time, not ours.

> She was an absolutely useless bitch. She was taking notice of what Social Services were telling her and not being independent.

> They believe what the social worker says.

These perceptions were also accompanied by uncertainty about the guardian's authority: parents commented that guardians were sometimes not allowed to speak in Social Services meetings and appeared to wield too little power in court to influence outcomes.

This seems a surprising finding given that many practitioners, including some guardians, are concerned that the guardian's opinion has too much influence on the court. This may reflect parents' inadequate comprehension of how the court process operates, in which case better explanations might help. Perhaps, however, the perception parents bring with them to the court, namely that Social Services are all powerful because they have experienced powerlessness, acts as such a strong distorting lens that other versions of reality become obscured.

The fact that guardians often support the local authority application, more so perhaps since the Children Act, of course serves to strengthen parents' views. It would be interesting to be able to test, through contemporaneous interviews, whether parental views about independence change significantly in the course of proceedings as the guardian's recommendations become apparent; there is certainly an indication that this is the case. Some parents with long involvement with Social Services also remembered individual guardians when they had formerly been social workers and were thus unshakeable in their conviction that since 'all social workers stick together' it was impossible for Guardians ad Litem to make impartial judgements.

On a more positive note there was some evidence that parental perceptions of the guardian were better when there had been a substantial amount of contact. One set of parents who said the guardian had only come to see them once were very insulted because:

> They only take a snapshot view of family life and this is what goes into their report.

There were a small number of other specific criticisms – for example, that guardians are overly intrusive: 'nothing but a private eye'. One guardian was said to have contacted both grandparents and a parent's employer against their wishes. Another parent complained that the guardian's assessment was:

> too much in favour of children; she wasn't looking at the family as a whole, just the kids. The law says keep the family together. If you want to have the best interests of the kids you've got to look at the father and mother too.

On the whole, however, it would seem parents understood the role of the guardian (20) and had received adequate explanations from guardians themselves. This is a significant improvement upon the experiences of parents during the infancy of the service as recorded in earlier research.[1] Most parents also made positive comments about the guardian's approach, such as 'honest', 'helpful' and 'supportive' and, most appreciated of all, 'a good listener'. Though we began this section pessimistically it is therefore appropriate to end with a selection of positive evaluations:

> She was excellent – I call her Mother Israel and she knows why I call her that.

> She was lovely, very caring and a good listener.

> She took no one's side: she thought about what the kids wanted and listened to me, more like a friend.

The judiciary

Finally, what did parents have to say about the judges and magistrates involved in their cases?

The first thing to note is the lack of continuity parents experienced among the judiciary hearing their cases. Change occurred in 19 of our 25 cases with one parent reporting having to go before four different judges. Such recollections of discontinuity were amply confirmed by our observation of court hearings and the worrying implications of this practice have been explored in the main report.

From their different perspective, most parents also placed a high premium on continuity. Where this was experienced, all but one expressed appreciation, familiarity appearing to enhance confidence and understanding of the decision-making process:

> It helped having the same one; it did matter.

Change was experienced as disruptive and time-wasting by 11 parents. Parents particularly resented the degree of recapping involved:

> We had different ones all the time, swapping and changing. It mattered because all the story had to be told all over again each time.

They were anxious about new people only getting a superficial view of the case by reading the documentation, 'because reading it is not the same as hearing' and losing the benefit of such personal rapport as had been established. They also expressed their underlying fear that different adjudicators might hold inconsistent views, fuelling their own uncertainties and fears as they approached the final hearing:

> We have had different ones and it is wrong. Because we had to keep changing,
> we felt that different magistrates might have different opinions.

These critical attitudes seemed to be held by parents irrespective of the outcome of their case; they appeared to be neither linked with nor skewed by loss of children, nor whether the case was heard by a magistrate or judge. The absence of any pattern suggests that parents were indeed making a fundamental criticism of the court system. Given the nature of these cases, high levels of consumer satisfaction are unlikely. However, it appears that a greater degree of judicial continuity might remove one source of legitimate and unavoidable dissatisfaction.

Of course there were a few parents who did not see discontinuity as a particular issue or who 'hadn't noticed'; six parents for whom it was actually seen as an advantage; and the mother mentioned earlier who would have dearly loved to get away from the judge who terrified her so much that she tried to hide away at the back of the court.

Parents who perceived having different members of the judiciary as advantageous felt a change midstream had had a positive effect on their case and that checks and balances had been kept in place, especially in regard to what they perceived Social Services were 'up to'. This kind of comment was usually expressed with some glee, especially if someone from the local authority appeared to have been rapped over the knuckles in the hearing. As one grandparent said openly: 'I was happy he told the local authority off.'

When it came to perceptions about the fairness and sensitivities of the judiciary involved in the cases, more parents were impressed (15) than otherwise (9). This might be considered surprising since they were the final arbiters, making decisions which often went against parents and that some parents came to court expecting to have their version of events vindicated.

It is true that a small number of parents were critical, either of the impartiality of those hearing their case or more frequently of their cold and impersonal approach. These parents commented for instance:

> He made some assumptions without hearing the other side of the story.
> It's like baking a cake without the egg.

> He was only doing his job but I thought he was against me.

> He was very cold. It was his manner, like he knew everything and I knew
> nothing.

It's a production line system.

Not a bit of love in the whole lot of them.

I felt like a leper.

In the main, however, judges and magistrates generally came in for only mild criticism which was quite outweighed by more positive assessments. Indeed one mother told us:

I thought they were all sensitive and fair. I liked all the judges.

Highest levels of satisfaction were expressed when the judiciary had directly addressed parents, listened patiently and sympathetically to what they had to say, shown an interest in the children and displayed respect, warmth and humanity. These qualities which, it has to be said, were associated more frequently with female members of the judiciary, were perhaps appreciated all the more because they had not been anticipated. For example, the sympathetic interest in family life symbolised by the judge who examined the family's photograph album probably went further to restore these particular parents' self-esteem than any other event in the process:

I wish there were more judges like her. She was like a mother with understanding and sensitivity.

These are not qualities which would be seen as critical to the performance of the judicial role in most other types of proceedings but this survey shows that they are clearly vital to judges and magistrates hearing these very difficult and sensitive family matters, a finding which has considerable implications for the selection and training of all members of the judiciary.

NOTES

[1] Murch M; Hunt J; Macleod A (1990): *Representation of the Child in the Civil Courts: Summary and Recommendations to the Department of Health*. Socio-Legal Centre for Family Studies, University of Bristol.

6 *The pace of court proceedings*

Perceptions of delay

One of the fundamental principles in the Children Act, stated for the first time in English law,[1] is that delay in the legal process is not normally in the interests of children. From our discussions with parents on this topic it appears that they, too, regard delay as an evil, contrary to their interests and having an inimical effect upon themselves and their families. Though we did not put the question directly to parents we would deduce that the general principle commands parental support.

From data collected in the main study we knew that the cases covered by this interview sample had lasted anything from nine weeks to 18 months, with a mean of 26 weeks and a median of 22. This accords very closely with the durations in the sample as a whole and chimes fairly well with parental recollections. The pace of proceedings was deemed to be 'about right' for only six families (four parents, two aunts). Most of these cases ended either in the children returning home or in a placement within the extended family and in the view of interviewees the time had been used constructively, enabling a thorough assessment to be undertaken before a decision was made:

> You had to give people time to investigate once it went to court. You can't rush it in case they misjudge. (Ten months, aunt)

> The delay was good because it gave us a chance for them to assess us in X [a residential placement]. (Six months, parent)

For two parents whose children were made subject to Care Orders and were to be placed for adoption, however, the three and four months respectively their cases were before the court was felt to be too short. Both these mothers had already lost other children to care. For one parent more time was needed to come to terms with a loss she saw as inevitable. The other considered that a slower pace might have affected the outcome, giving her the opportunity to break with her violent partner and demonstrate her determination to do so permanently;

> If the case had been longer still they would have really known that I wasn't getting back with him and I might have had the kids back.

Three parents were inclined to think that their case had dragged on rather a long time, but were unsure as to whether that could be considered too long or par for the course:

> I didn't know whether that was really long. How long is it supposed to take? (Four months)

The majority of interviewees (16), however, were much less diffident:

> It should have lasted three to four months at the most instead of eight months.

> They dragged it out too long. It could have been sorted out well before that. (12 months)

> It was too long. Social Services kept delaying it. (Ten months)

> It was hanged out, they kept adjourning it. (Four months)

One father in particular was cynical about the whole legal process, of which, it must be said, he had not inconsiderable experience:

> Everything takes a long time in law, not only in children's cases. They are all lazy: they could use information technology and in 24 hours you can do a lot of things.

In general, however, the reasons parents gave for proceedings having been delayed generally seemed to match realistically our knowledge of events, suggesting they were well-informed about this aspect of the process at least. The main factors they cited are all too familiar to practitioners, namely:

- assessments, often involving a residential placement;
- additional evidence from experts or other professionals;
- late evidence;
- applications from new parties, particularly relatives;
- contact issues unresolved at the time of the substantive hearing of the care application;
- significant changes in family circumstances;
- concurrent criminal proceedings; and
- the difficulty of gathering all the parties, professionals and legal representatives together at a time which did not clash with other commitments, holidays and sick leave.

Although parents may have comprehended the reasons for delay, that does not mean they were understanding of them. On the contrary, they were often highly critical of practical difficulties arising from conflicting professional commitments, for example, or tardiness in producing reports or arranging assessments; and the number of experts and other witnesses called by the local authority. Some parents whose children had been accommodated prior to proceedings, already angry about the escalation of action, were also suspicious that delay had been contrived by Social Services, another tactic to strengthen the case against them.

Only two solicitors were reported to have been successful in expediting matters. In the main, parents perceived their lawyers to be largely impotent in influencing the pace of events – whether this was to speed things up, or, on occasions, slow things down.

> They ignored her basically.

> She wanted it shortened but it didn't help because they took no notice of her.

> We tried to speed it up but there was nothing he could give the court as ammunition.

Perhaps surprisingly, lawyer ineffectualness in this regard was not held against them, nor did it provoke questions about professional competence. Rather, again and again parents said 'he was trying to do his best'.

The impact of delay

It is difficult, of course, to separate the effects upon parents of proceedings from the effects of delay in completing those proceedings. Universally, parents found the period while their case was before the court 'awful', 'very difficult', 'horrible'. Most 'just wanted to get it over with'. As described earlier, however, most parents did not find it easier to cope as time went on, indeed for many, things became worse. Delay, it would seem, amplifies, rather than changes, the generally negative impact of proceedings upon families. Parents, children (including those not subject to proceedings), even the extended family may all be affected to varying degrees.

When asked about the consequences of delay for themselves parents identified three main problems: the prolongation of emotional distress, their inability to plan for the future and the disruption in their relationship with the child.

The majority of parents described feeling very angry, upset, depressed or inadequate throughout the duration of their court case. Five were so distressed that they sought psychiatric help or counselling, including a father in prison who was desperate because:

> I can't talk to other prisoners about my feelings – you don't really have friends in here. I was going mad, accommodating hate.

A number of parents already suffering mental health problems reported that the delay in resolving proceedings undermined their recovery. One mother with schizophrenia told us:

> It made me go haywire. I was a pressure cooker. You come home, think about it, wake up thinking about it. It was too much for me.

These feelings of acute distress were reiterated by another mother who had suffered a severe psychotic breakdown:

> I found it unbearable and I couldn't get well until she was back.

Delay prolonged the insecurity and uncertainty of a period in which parents perceived themselves to be 'in limbo', with their children usually away from home and their eventual return at issue. Fearful of giving themselves false expectations, parents hesitated in doing practical things such as redecorating a child's bedroom, while the longer a case went on, the more the prospect of return seemed to fade. (In reality, the research data seems to suggest, this is not the case, indeed some of the longest cases were those where children were returned home or were placed with relatives, while those ending in permanent separation were often the quickest.) Parental perceptions in this regard however highlight the fact that no one took a favourable outcome for granted even when things appeared to be proceeding their way. There is an interesting parallel with the anxiety many adoptive parents feel right up to the point the order is made, even if the birth parents are not contesting and none of the professionals have any doubts about the placement.[2]

Finally, delay increased parental difficulties both in coping with separation from their children in care and managing their relationships with those children, particularly when the outcome of the case was uncertain:

> It had an effect on me because I was unsure what was happening with her. Contact was not good because I didn't know where I was going with her.

In the next chapter we look in more detail at what parents had to say about interim placements and their experience of interim contact.

NOTES

[1] Section 1 (2).

[2] Murch M; Lowe N; Borkowski M; Copner R; Griew K (1993): *Pathways to Adoption*. HMSO.

7 *The interim period*

Interim placements

For the majority of parents in the interview sample, care proceedings meant at least a period of separation from their children. There were only two cases where the children remained at home throughout and five where parent(s) and children were together in a residential placement.

The need for removal was questioned by quite a few of the parents interviewed, who urged that while the matter was before the court children should remain at home, if necessary under close supervision:

> Courts should give a trial period to parents and children without taking them away.

This, they considered, would afford them an opportunity to prove themselves without the fracturing of relationships and the trauma of subsequent return. Moreover, as described earlier, some parents recognised that they had foolishly disregarded earlier warnings about possible legal action. They argued that, another chance, within the context of proceedings, would allow them to demonstrate that the shock of court action and the potential loss of the children had indeed brought them to their senses and galvanised them into making efforts to show that they could parent effectively.

By far the commonest type of out-of-home placement was a non-related foster home (18 cases) although some children also spent time in hospital (three) or in a children's home (two). Some children experienced more than one form of placement.

Almost unanimously parents claimed they had not been consulted nor given any choice of placement (22 out of 23 cases). The exception, given the options of a residential mother and baby home and a foster home, chose the former. The family subsequently returned to the community with the child on a Care Order. However, although the majority of parents told us 'there was no say at all'; 'no, none at all', this was not necessarily as alienating for them as might have been predicted. None of the parents specifically challenged this aspect of their case; indeed it seems they had not expected any such consultation.

It seems parents are rather more likely to have been consulted about any special needs their children might have. As we describe elsewhere[1] many of the children in the study suffered from a range of chronic if sometimes minor health conditions traditionally associated with lower socio-economic groupings.[2] Parents mentioned 'glue ear' and other hearing difficulties; eye problems such as squints; chest complaints including asthma; eczema; or eating problems. A number of children had special educational needs or emotional or behavioural problems. Two babies were born addicted to drugs and four suffered from other serious medical conditions.

The parents who said they had been consulted about their children's difficulties (ten cases) were impressed that they had been shown this degree of respect which helped in some measure to mitigate their otherwise adverse perceptions. Clearly this is an area in which changes in practice would be relatively easy to implement, non-controversial and might help to improve relationships between parent and agency.

The racial, linguistic, cultural and religious needs of looked-after children are factors the local authority is now required to take into account. This was a major issue for the ethnic minority families in this study, although not always in the ways that might have been anticipated. Two mothers of Afro-Caribbean origin, for instance, whose children had been placed with black foster parents, both stated they would have preferred their children to have been placed in loving white foster homes, one primarily because this would have enabled them to remain with a familiar person:

> White or black – I'm not prejudiced. I'd rather they were with Jenny than a black person that I didn't know. The children are British born and so am I. I'm not Afro-Caribbean just because my Mum was born in Jamaica.

The other mother told us:

> I don't know about all this race stuff. As long as the couple are all right is all I'm bothered about. I can't take too much 'black' really around me. I'm for mixed black and white. All black can actually be bitchy.

Another mother who had been ostracised by her family and her community was petrified that her child would be placed in a culturally appropriate placement with Asian foster carers, where she might be exposed to further vilification.

Two other families were critical of the assumptions that appear to have been made about the commonality of cultures. In the first a Nigerian child was placed in an Afro-Caribbean household and exposed to what both his mother and his aunt saw as a total clash of lifestyles and values. Again a white family, it was said, would have been preferable to an inappropriate, black placement. In the second case, relationships between the family and the agency were soured from the beginning when the father, who was of mixed race and of Mediterranean complexion, was described as 'black' before the social worker had even met him:

> I was born in X country, of mixed race, but am still white. They said I was black and even put it in the Children's Report. It really got up my nose because I have always been British and the social worker hadn't even seen me and told the foster parent I was black too.

As his wife pointed out:

> It was a bad start, as my husband was insulted over the ethnic issue and this became paramount. They never apologised in court for the mix-up and it didn't help the blaming that went on between my husband and myself. I have two little white children born in this city. If it comes to the crunch I am from a different part of the UK, Gaelic speaking, and all this ethnic categorisation should be no big thing.

Getting it wrong in a different way also produced complaints. Thus one Muslim child:

> was given food she shouldn't have had such as pork. The foster parent said she did not have time to cook separate meals for her, even though I was providing her with special meat. They weren't very good carers.

Another child was placed in a household where the white foster parents were unmarried, contrary to traditional Muslim values, while parents who were devout Christians complained about the disregard of their request for the children to be looked after in a practising Christian household:

> I don't think Social Services took any notice of our wishes. We often went out a lot including to church with them. We want the children baptised but Social Services won't help us in arranging a date. The foster mum doesn't take them to church.

The lessons which seem to emerge from all this is that we are dealing with a set of complex perceptions and attitudes, where prejudgements on the part of practitioners may prove unhelpful, unwise and sometimes erroneous. Questions of identify and the identification with a particular group may not be self-evident, and each decision needs to be taken in consultation with families in the context of their belief systems, traditions, degree of assimilation and personal preferences.

It is important to note, however, that there were only four cases in which the issue of inappropriate matching subsumed all other perceptions. Moreover there were surprisingly few complaints about the *quality* of foster care even in the interview sample as a whole. (One parent, for instance, complained that the foster carers were intolerant of the needs of young children, citing their 'pickiness' with food; another that the foster parents were siphoning off money which should have been spent on food and clothing for the children.)

Most complaints, however, were situational: siblings being separated, undesirable influences from older foster children, distance from home, disruption to the children's lives through moving school and neighbourhoods. One set of parents had expressed concern about the potential disruption to their children's education as the result of a proposed change of school. The local authority funded special transport, which however then involved the children in a lot of travelling and as their mother pointed out quite correctly 'made the day very long for them'.

One might have expected parents whose own standards of care was being called into question to be inclined to be hyper-critical of the foster carers themselves. This was emphatically not the case. Most parents spoke very warmly about the foster carers, some of whom were still caring for the children at the time of interview:

> They were a very loving nice older couple, a close family with grown up kids who used to play with my children.

> They seemed nice people. They were nearby and I was able to phone.

> I have a good working relationship with them after a few hiccups: one was about the pronunciation of [X's] name. They get good care.

> I'm happy. I know the foster mum personally. She is a nice person and the child is happy.

These and similar accolades are a tribute not only to the foster carers themselves, but to the parents who were able to distinguish between their feelings about the process which had led to their children being cared for by others, and the individuals providing that care. Small kindnesses and sensitivities seemed to mean a great deal. One mother, for instance, told us:

> The foster mum is all right. She asked me if I minded Jane's ears being pierced. I thought it was very nice of her to ask me.

Such marks of respect helped to mitigate, if only in a small way, the acute pain these often very distressed parents continued to feel throughout their period of separation:

> It was a bit difficult in my position, I used to cry about her, and wanted to care for her myself.

> It's all very difficult when children get attached to their foster carer.

As other research studies have found, such feelings can mean that parents have to nerve themselves for every contact visit and that sometimes not visiting is more tolerable. It is to the issue of contact that we now turn.

Interim contact

In contrast to the relatively high level of satisfaction expressed about placement arrangements the majority of parents were dissatisfied with some aspect of their contact during this interim period.

Only seven parents, for instance, considered that the amount of contact was about right in their circumstances, most complaining it was too infrequent and failed to take adequate account of symbolic occasions such as Christmas and birthdays. Distance was a problem in six cases with parents recounting similar difficulties with the cost and infrequency of public transport as those that (it will be recalled) beset their attempts to get to court hearings. It was also again notable that parents who reported having been assisted with transport (seven cases) were grateful for this help although two mothers reported being too proud to accept an offer of financial assistance and one being afraid to ask 'because they would think I am relying on them all the time'.

> It was hard for me to see her, a long way and distressing. I used to cry going down the road, feel depressed because I couldn't take her home. It wasn't easy.

> It's hard to tell whether he likes me. He likes the sweeties I take!

Above all, however, as the above comments illustrate, parents were distressed by the experience of contact. They reported variously struggling with their own reactions to separation which resurfaced at each visit; feeling prematurely dispossessed and fearful that their child was becoming attached to the foster carer and might not even recognise them; being afraid that each visit might be the last. Under these strains they found that much of the spontaneity had gone out of their interactions with their children.

This was exacerbated by the conditions under which contact often took place. Parents whose children were brought to see them in prison were undoubtedly struggling with the most artificial and restricted environment, in which contact had become a public spectacle:[3]

> I was not happy with the time allowed and being supervised is embarrassing. My friends in prison were saying 'Is that your baby?' It looked like I didn't know her when she was screaming, it was really shameful.

> I would have liked more visits but I understand the circumstances in prison. We had to beg the Governor. Prison is something else. Everyone was there, three to four screws, the social worker, the foster mother. It was very embarrassing and there was no privacy.

Sadly, however, these feelings of shame, embarrassment, lack of privacy and artificiality were not confined to parents in these particularly unfortunate circumstances.

> I was never allowed to see the children at home. I always had to see them at the foster mum's where I was watched all the time. You can't treat kids like kids when someone is watching you. I used to play football and swings with them in the garden, but when your backs turned they [i.e. the social worker and foster carer] were indoors having a good natter about you and peeping out of the window half the time.

Unequivocally parents hated being supervised, whether this was formal or covert:

> Supervision is terrible – so artificial. It neither does the child nor the parent any good.

> Supervision is very bad. The social worker never left us alone with the children. It made us very ill at ease. There was no privacy either. Now we've got a room of our own but it took a long while to convince them.

Some expressed resentment at not being able to see the children at home or even take them out of the placement:

> I wanted my children to come and visit me at home. [Social Services] took them, so they should have brought them to see me. They took them and if they can't find the facility for them to visit me, the kids have to suffer and it's Social Services' fault!

> I was not allowed to take him out on my own, not even down the street.

Given the circumstances of some of these cases it might be hard to accede to parents' requests for home visits – particularly if resources cannot be made available for the supervision which might make it safe. Equally the needs of parents in this respect may conflict with the needs of children. For some children a home visit could resurrect old fears or hold out a prospect of return which might be either unwelcome or unrealistic. However, there may be cases where it could be considered more actively.

Similarly the research suggests supervised contact may be overused. Clearly there will be situations when there may be justified fears for the child's physical safety, though they would seem to be rare, or concern that the child may be put under emotional pressure. Sometimes, however, it seemed to the research team that parents were not being monitored for either of these reasons but as a means of assessing parent–child interaction. Given the artificiality of the situations in which contact takes place the value of this is questionable and may be quite outweighed by the damage such monitoring may inflict on parent–child relationships already under severe strain.

It is clear that despite their often complimentary comments about the foster placement itself, many parents would prefer contact to take place elsewhere. The use of properly equipped contact centres, with staff who are trained to support parents and facilitate contact (such as are available in some localities) may thus be one way forward. Where monitoring is considered vital for the child's safety it is also possible that parents would find video surveillance or one-way screens more acceptable and less intrusive than the physical presence of a supervisor.

Clearly such a suggestion has considerable resource implications and the advantages and disadvantages for the child would have to be carefully considered in each case. We would urge, however, that it be seriously considered. The quality of contact is often a key factor in decision-making in care cases and reports on contact sessions frequently form part of the local authority evidence. At the moment it seems parents may, however unintentionally, be being set up to fail.

Sadly only eight parents found social workers to be understanding of their difficulties in relation to contact, with epithets such as 'unhelpful', 'uncaring', 'unsympathetic' being used disappointingly often:

> They don't care. If they really cared they would have provided transport to get me there.

> I suffer from anxiety attacks outside the house but they said I was too lazy to bother. That is what they are like – scum!

> I don't think they give a damn.

The social workers involved in these cases, may, of course, place an entirely different construction upon events. *Prima facie*, however, such comments are worrying. Taken together with everything reported here they suggest that the accumulation of knowledge since contact issues were highlighted in research in the 1980s[4] has had less impact than might have been expected or hoped for.

The need for Interim Contact Orders

Whilst parents spoke freely about the difficulties surrounding contact it proved very difficult to ascertain from them to what extent the court had been involved in the regulation of contact. Some parents were confused as to whether any interim orders had been made at all, others as to the details, while arrangements could also vary in the course of the case. Even when no formal order is made, the proposed arrangements may be put to the court, which might explain this rather confusing statement from one father:

> The court laid it out for three visits a week. We would have preferred a court order.

In so far as we can judge, however, parents with voluntary contact arrangements did not seem to feel the need for court regulation, while those who understood that the court had been involved in some way very much wanted this measure of protection. This suggests both that orders are not being made routinely and that, in this respect at least, parents enjoyed the level of court control they required, a very satisfactory finding, even if one in which we are not totally confident, because of the lack of clarity and precision in some of the interview material.

The reasons for preferring a Contact Order, in contrast, were quite clear and related to parents' lack of trust in Social Services. Without an order, they felt, arrangements might have fallen foul of the whims of prejudiced social workers, lack of resources and general muddle:

> I preferred the court keeping a Contact Order on her as Social Services made excuses about her settling down properly. No – definitely not arrangements with Social Services. I probably would never have seen her if it was down to them because I don't think the social worker I've got wanted me to have her back at all.

The court was therefore seen as more impartial and most crucially, able to exercise control over the behaviour of the agency.

A formal Contact Order may also be more acceptable to relatives with care. Three of the four relatives interviewed in this situation told us they felt an order provided better protection for themselves and the children against undue interference and conflict with difficult parents.

The need for Interim Care Orders

On the whole, therefore, the role of the court in regulating interim contact was seen by parents as a means of upholding their rights and thus something to be desired. Interim Care Orders, of course, have quite a different function in that they deprive parents of their right to decide where and with whom their child shall live or to remove them from an out-of-home placement.

For this reason again three out of four relative carers were very happy to have the security of an order:

> Yes, it was a good thing there was an order. The mother even snatched the child after the Care Order was made so I was happy to be closely supervised.

> It was necessary for Mum because she would have tried to do things her way and would have tried to see them more often and make a nuisance of herself.

A small number of parents also freely admitted that they could not have been trusted without an order:

> I would have kidnapped them and taken them abroad, to Australia or somewhere.

It was necessary in my bloody case. If I'd snatched her it would have brought more problems on my head.

One mother told us that she would have been prepared to comply with voluntary arrangements; her husband, however, who was very much the dominant partner in the relationship, would not.

The majority of parents whose children were subject to such orders, however, considered that Interim Care Orders had been heavy-handed. This was particularly the case where children had been accommodated prior to proceedings, where parents expressed some confusion as to the sudden need for compulsion when they felt they had co-operated in the past and demonstrated their trustworthiness. Parents who might have been tempted to remove the children also told us that the authority of the court and the likely consequences if they reneged upon agreements, was sufficient control:

> They didn't trust me not to take them back. But I know that is against the law and I wouldn't have done it.

> They were thinking I might take him but it would have been kidnapping him.

Finally, a number of parents talked in terms of their child's needs in the situation, of a wish to protect them from further disruption or put them at risk:

> I would have left her with the foster mother anyway. I think moving her would have upset her, lots of moves might mean she would turn out backward: she'd play up a bit more.

> I thought it was stupid really. I wouldn't take him as he was settled there.

> I would have left her there as I was worried about [my partner's] violence as he was on bail at the time.

> I would have preferred it if they had not made an order. I would have left her until I got better.

Practitioners, of course, may wish to take all this with an extremely large pinch of salt. Care proceedings are often initiated precisely because parents have not been able to work on a voluntary basis. We would suggest, however, that the fact that the case is before the court may mean that voluntary arrangements automatically carry a greater degree of authority. Parents know, and their lawyers will almost certainly emphasise to them, that defaulting on such an agreement, even when there is no formal sanction, will bode extremely ill for their case. So unless parents feel they have nothing to lose or are too erratic or disturbed to be able to stick to the agreed terms, most could be expected to comply.

We would suggest that the use of parental undertakings might be one way of ensuring the security of a placement while giving parents the sense that they are partners in a contractual, rather than a coercive, arrangement. The instrumental value of at least formal co-operation is a lesson that by this stage often seems to have gone home and there was some sign of the softening of attitudes. Thus there may be an opportunity, however slight, for beginning to develop a more constructive partnership.

Such opportunities may also arise as the result of changes in the circumstances of the families involved, which, as we shall see in the next section, can be considerable.

Changing circumstances

Other researchers[5] have graphically exposed the fallacy of assuming that the situations to which children 'return' when they leave care are essentially the same as those they left. The same point has to be made about families involved in care proceedings. The extent of the turbulence revealed in our main study is amply confirmed by the families we interviewed, 22 of whom cited substantial changes in circumstances and lifestyle. These included:

- changes of partner (8);
- changes in accommodation (7);
- improvements or deterioration in parental mental ill health or addiction (5);
- criminal proceedings (5);
- birth of other children (4);
- changes in employment status (2); and
- allegation of further abuse (1).

Some of these changes flowed from the initiation of court action; others had an effect upon the progress of proceedings. Sometimes both effects were reported. One mother, for instance, who had eventually found the courage to report her cohabitee's abuse of her youngest child, took out an injunction against him and moved to be near her own family. In the light of the changed circumstances Social Services began the rehabilitation process. Mother then became pregnant by a new partner whom she proposed to marry and proceedings were delayed while he was checked out.

Participation in welfare decision-making

Most parents recalled being invited to at least one meeting with Social Services during this interim period, ranging from case conferences, reviews and planning meetings on Social Services' premises to smaller, less formal meetings in, for example, a foster home. For the most part parents attended these meetings alone and unsupported and while all the parents were legally represented by this stage only two were accompanied by their lawyer. The adverse comments parents made about the extent of their true participation in pre-court meetings generally holds true for those they attended while proceedings were in train and will not be repeated here. Many of the estranged fathers and other relatives interviewed remained aggrieved that, as far as they could see, they were still being overlooked.

Another recurring theme was parental impotence to influence events. The majority of the parents interviewed (17 cases) told us they felt their own suggestions for the future had not been taken seriously and their ability to deflect Social Services from their pre-set track was poor. These highly dissatisfied case families once again talked of their own capitulation in the face of the system, of feeling coerced by Social Services, of their fear of being 'wrong-footed' or making things worse by appearing uncooperative:

> We felt right under pressure without a doubt. They wanted this, they wanted that, not what we wanted. In other words they still didn't trust us.

> I would have agreed to anything as long as the children were with me.

Parents who felt they had made every effort to meet Social Services' demands and still lost their children, were particularly bitter or angry, and felt also that their personal integrity had been impugned by harsh judgements and lack of understanding of their personal difficulties:

> They all thought I would take my husband back again, but no way, when I discovered he was a paedophile. They didn't believe me but I had years of hell. I was told I couldn't fight for them, I'd lost them anyway and that's the way it ended. I caved in although I felt like setting light to the place.

> I wasn't drinking anymore but the Social Services always put a question mark over that.

It is important to note, however, that such feelings were not confined to parents who had lost their children and who might understandably be expected to feel bitter. A majority of the parents who might be regarded as having good outcomes were also scathing about the degree of participation and consultation and the scant regard paid to their suggestions. For these parents too, partnership in decision-making was still a sham.

Nonetheless, there were a few glimmers of light in an otherwise gloomy picture with eight parents and four relatives (albeit all with successful outcomes) feeling they had been included in decision-making and exercised some influence over the way things developed. One mother with some experience of pre-Act practice told us:

> Yes, they took my views seriously. Things were being questioned all the way along the line; lots of changing views and circumstances and I was coping better. It was much better done like this.

This satisfied mother had experienced a number of changes in her favour including getting rid of her partner, the alleged perpetrator and moving to new accommodation. These changes, which permitted a reassessment of her parenting, meant that the children were returned, a favourable outcome. In the next chapter we reach the end of the court process and examine how the other families in the sample fared.

NOTES

[1] Hunt J; Macleod A (1998): *The Last Resort: Child Protection, the Courts and the 1989 Children Act*. The Stationery Office.

[2] Bebbington A; Miles J (1989): 'The background of children who enter local authority care'. *British Journal of Social Work*, 19, pp 349–68. Brown M; Madge N (1982): *Despite the Welfare State*. Heinemann. Wadsworth MEJ (1991): *The Imprint of Time. Childhood History and Adult Life*. Clarendon.

[3] Further discussion of some of these issues can be found in: Peckham A (1985): *A Woman in Custody*. Fontana. Carlen P (1989): *Women's Imprisonment – a Strategy of Abolition*. Centre for Criminology, University of Keele.

[4] Milham S; Bullock R; Hosie K; Haak M (1986): *Lost in Care: the Problems of Maintaining Links between Children in Care and their Families*. Gower.

[5] Bullock R; Little M; Milham S (1993): *Going Home*. Dartmouth Press. Farmer E; Parker R (1991): *Trials and Tribulations: Returning Children from Local Authority Care to their Families*. HMSO. Stein M; Carey K (1986): *Leaving Care*. Basil Blackwell.

8 *The outcome of proceedings*

Hopes, fears and realities

One of the striking findings to emerge from our research on the sample as a whole was the small proportion of cases in which, at the point of initiating proceedings, Social Services were clear about their long-term objectives. Objectives were most likely to be contingent in cases which were relatively unknown but even in this interview sample of mainly long-term families there were only nine in which objectives appeared to be fixed. In two the plan was for the children to be supervised at home, so only seven started off with the firm intention of placing the children in long-term substitute care.

The degree to which Social Services see the outcome of proceedings being contingent upon developments in the course of proceedings, however, will not necessarily be made explicit to parents. Nor will this be readily apparent from the formal structure of proceedings by which Social Services do not simply put the matter in the court forum, they make an application for an order. Thus when asked what their understanding of Social Services' intentions were at the start of proceedings the majority of parents (20) recalled that Care Orders would be sought at the end of the day and only five considered that the return of their children was being contemplated.

In one sense, therefore, parents may go through proceedings not only carrying an unnecessary burden of anxiety, but also convinced that Social Services are more immovable than in fact may be the case. It may even be possible that if the true situation were more fully explained parents might feel inclined to make more effort to change or at least feel they had enjoyed a greater degree of participation in the process. On the other hand, one could say that parents were at least accurate in their assessment that the outcome of care proceedings could well be Care Orders and permanent separation so that their pessimism was both legitimate and self-protecting.

As the legal process grinds on and options are explored and discarded, it usually becomes clearer how the land lies. Negotiations with Social Services, perhaps as the result of the changes outlined in the last chapter, may mean that there is no longer a dispute. Alternatively if there have been contested interim hearings parents may have a glimmer of which way the final hearing may go or may have been told about the recommendation of the Guardian ad Litem. By the time of the final hearing, our experience of care cases suggests, few cases are genuinely borderline, even if the rules of the game usually forbid any explicit recognition of this.

As a result, in the majority of the sample cases the eventual outcome was as parents expected even if not necessarily as they had hoped. Nine families, however, appeared to have been unprepared. When the outcome was also unfavourable, as was usually but not invariably the case, they were, as a result, even more distressed.

Responses to the legal outcome

Ten of our 25 interview cases had outcomes which were broadly satisfactory to the parents concerned: five ended in the local authority withdrawing the application, two with supervision orders and three with Care Orders with an intention to rehabilitate. These interviewees generally initially summed up their emotions in words such as 'happy', 'fine', 'we felt we had won'. However, while they often described themselves as more ready to co-operate with Social Services in the future there was a clear sense, illustrated in the comments below, that this had been forced on them by an appreciation of the alternatives:

> If you don't agree, you don't get your child back.

> I really went along with it because she was coming home eventually – otherwise I would have tried to fight it.

Similarly, parents had very mixed feelings about Social Services having a continuing role in their lives, which was still construed as interference:

> The Supervision Order meant the social worker had to come in and check everything was all right once a week. I wasn't keen on that.

The sense that children were returning home almost on loan, which was evident in some of the interviews, was explicitly voiced by one mother who told us:

> I saw the Care Order as a time of looking after her for Social Services, in a way. You have got to check everything with them, like taking her on holiday. It is just like you are looking after her. The only thing I say good about it was that she was going to be returned home.

Parents were correct of course that the intention of the Children Act is to be clear that when a Care Order is made parental responsibility is shared between the parents and the local authority. But this was intended to ensure that parents with children who are looked after continue to take a full part in their children's lives, not that somehow children who return home assume an uncertain and uneasy status. If this is the message unwittingly conveyed to parents there would be grounds for anxiety that such children will become treated as 'spoilt'[1] with all that that implies for their future within the family. This is one issue it may be possible to explore further in our follow-up study.[2]

If parents with favourable outcomes were ambivalent, the remaining parents reported violent initial reactions of anger, disbelief, despair or hatred with often an overwhelming desire to hit out:

> I literally hated them. I felt like setting light to the place.

> I felt like smacking [the social worker] in the face.

One mother, describing how she had become 'so angry, I went mad' lashed out at the guardian and had to be restrained. While the vehemence of these feelings may have become slightly muted over time very few of the parents we interviewed, which was usually several months after the completion of proceedings, were able to accept the court decision without a sense of bitterness or anger. As one mother said sadly:

> I expected it. But I couldn't accept it and I still can't now.

Parents, it would seem, need more assistance than they currently get in coping with this agonising experience and coming to terms with the inevitable. We do not suggest that practitioners are so inhuman as to abandon parents to their distress but sometimes, it seems, that is what it feels like. Social workers, of course, are probably the last people parents ever want to see again, but there may be nobody else. Solicitors can mop up the tears outside court but then usually disappear from parents' lives onto the next case. Yet again, therefore, it seems there is a need for some form of identified, neutral, non-judgemental support.

Parental comprehension of the court's decision

By the time of the research interview almost all the parents and relatives seen were well-informed about the orders made by the court and their implications and were able to explain these to the researchers without prompting.

There did appear however to be some misunderstandings about the nature of a Care Order. One couple had understood the order was automatically reviewed after six months:

> I was shocked because I was under the impression that you went back to court every six months until you proved yourself. I thought it was an ongoing thing and we would win next time, I didn't realise at the time we had lost the children.

In most cases, however, parental misapprehensions concerned the effect of the order upon their continuing role. We have already referred to parents feeling in a different relationship to children 'on loan' from Social Services and perhaps having their sense of parental responsibility diminished. This was even more marked where children were not to return:

> I realised I wasn't their mum anymore and Social Services have power to decide everything in her life.

> The Care Order meant he is not mine any more.

> It meant the baby was going into care and she was no longer my own and we had no say in anything.

It would therefore appear that the fundamental principle emphasised so much in the Children Act, that while a Care Order gives the local authority parental responsibility it does not take it away from parents, had not percolated through at least to these parents. What they correctly perceived was that Social Services were going to be in the driving seat; the notion that they might even be in the car was foreign to them.

The research interviews were, of course, carried out some time after proceedings had been completed, when parents had had opportunity to clarify what was decided and what it meant. Thinking back, however, to the time when they sat in court and heard the 'verdict' being pronounced, most described being in such a state of emotional turmoil they could not properly take in what was being said. This was sometimes compounded by the complexity of the language used or poor acoustics. In four cases parents had not understood what the final order was and had to check with their solicitor. Others told us:

> At the summing up, I couldn't absorb it, such a blur.

> I can't remember what he said. All I can remember is I felt like shouting out.

> I didn't hear a lot of what he said. It had been a long day and I was totally exhausted.

> I couldn't understand anything as I hardly went to school.

What parents did take in was whether or not they had 'lost' their children:

> I just knew I was getting her back.

> It meant I had been co-operating with the care plan and they were returning her home to me.

> It meant all my kids were put up for adoption. I've lost them anyway, that's the way it ended.

> It meant he had to go to a foster home and we mustn't take him away from it.

Other key parts of the judgement remained imprinted on some parental memories:

> It was still alcoholism.

> My husband was a paedophile.

> What my past was like, my failure to report my husband's behaviour.

However while parents in 14 cases could recall the court giving reasons for the decision, for the most part, as we have seen, they were lost on them:

> I think the judge did explain properly but I was a bit confused.

The requirement for magistrates to give reasons for their decisions was an important procedural innovation under the Children Act, bringing the Family Proceedings Court process more into line with the higher courts where judgements will be given in court in contested cases. We would concur that carefully worded clear judgements are important to parents: in demonstrating the court's impartiality and the fairness of the adjudication; in helping parents make sense of the decision and come to terms with its implication so that they can reconstruct their lives; in encouraging them to work co-operatively with practitioners in the future; and finally simply as a symbol of personal respect.

Clearly, however, it is not enough for explanations to be read out in court. Parents need something in writing which they can read, digest and if necessary ask about, once the immediate turmoil which inevitably accompanies the final hearing has died down. We consider this should be provided by the court and that it should be a recognised (and funded) part of the solicitor's task to go through this document with the parent and ensure that they understand the reasons for the court's decision and the meaning and implications of any orders made. At the moment, if the parents we interviewed had accurate recall, few seemed to have received even a copy of the order.

Perceptions of justice

Perhaps rather surprisingly, considering their other criticisms of the legal process, parents in 15 cases acknowledged that they had been treated fairly and justly. Even more surprising was the fact that this was not entirely dependent upon outcome.

Parents who lost their children as the result of care proceedings might be expected to feel that the process had been unfair and certainly many did:

> It was disgusting, stupid and unfair.

> Totally unfair and completely out of order.

> We weren't given a chance.

However in five of the 15 cases with unfavourable outcomes parents seemed to be satisfied, even if rather grudgingly, that the legal process had been essentially fair. One might speculate, of course, that the continuing scapegoating of Social Services by these parents may have served to absorb and deflect their wrath at the decision. None the less, such an unexpected finding gives some grounds for confidence that the judicial system retains a measure of credibility for such disadvantaged parents even if the process remains in so many respects alien and alienating.

Picking up the pieces

Whatever the outcome, court proceedings leave their mark upon parents, who in the aftermath of legal action are usually left in a state of emotional turmoil, sometimes even amounting to trauma. As we neared the end of the research interview and moved onto subsequent events, parents vividly described a maelstrom of feelings including anger, resentment, sadness, confusion, insecurity, shame and guilt.

The majority of parents whose children had been returned, or who had other children at home, reported feeling their family life had been disrupted and themselves usurped and deskilled in their parenting role. Their sense of being under constant scrutiny made them nervous or unnatural in their everyday interactions lest one slip should result in renewed action:

> Whatever happens, if they have an accident, they would say I had done it on purpose.

> We've still got one child. They're not having him. I'm worried and tense and fearful that they will find something wrong with him.

Yet, as other researchers have described,[3] some of the difficulties which returned children were presenting meant that parents were placed under more than normal pressure. One mother, for instance, rather worryingly told us:

> Sometimes I bloody well wish she was still in care; after nine months at home I thought she would settle down but she wakes up a lot at night and is always biting people.

Enabling parents to cope with such difficulties, to re-build their relationships with returned children and re-establish confidence in their parenting is no easy task when the main helping agency is still seen as responsible for the court action and on the alert for signs of failure. Moreover, as reported earlier, most parents considered the court action unnecessary and there was very little congruence between their perspective and the agency's on the seriousness of the concerns. The foundations for effective work must therefore be somewhat shaky. In such a context the task of rehabilitation which goes beyond ensuring protection from further harm to promoting the welfare of the child within his/her family may best be supported by bringing in another agency less contaminated by the statutory intervention.

Parents whose children had been committed to care were struggling to come to terms with their loss, describing to us how they felt:

> Lonely, empty, nothing to live for. The only reason I am here still is that at the moment the kids still live in this city.

> Upset, depressed, fed up.

> Sad, confused and angry.

It did not appear from our interviews that parents were necessarily receiving help with what is essentially a grieving process. Again this is a role which is very difficult for the social worker to fulfil, as they will almost certainly be identified as the agent of loss, but which needs to be provided by someone with relevant skills.

In some of these cases, of course, by the stage of the research interview, contact with the children had already been terminated and parents had had to face up to the reality of a sudden break in their relationship. Others, however, described the prolonged agony of a slow weakening of links as children became more attached to their current carers and they seemed to be 'drifting further and further away' and the difficulties of explaining to the children why they could not return home.

All parents had to make their own personal accommodation to what had happened. They also had to deal with the repercussions on their intimate relationships as even previously stable partnerships were rocked by recriminations and suspicion. In this unhappy situation only a few were able to rely unreservedly on help from relatives as even those who were in contact with their extended families prior to proceedings most often reported a drastic deterioration in relationships (52%). Some parents strove desperately to keep their families in the dark; others had to cope with angry reactions and expressions of family shame while in some cases sides had become polarised. In a small number of cases, of course, it had been relatives who had alerted Social Services to the condition of the children in the first place.

Fear of exposure to the reaction of the wider community meant that some parents had also striven to keep their own counsel and were accordingly very distressed when somehow word of their troubles got out, in two cases getting into the media, where although their names were not given, their identity was not difficult to establish:

> It was in the paper and on the local TV. The neighbours stopped being friends with me and the whole street knew about it.

There were only two cases in which neighbours were said to have remained friendly. More commonly parents felt themselves to have become avoided and the object of malicious gossip. Three parents from ethnic minority groups also described acute feelings of cultural shame, feeling disgraced within their communities and subject to a real degree of ostracism.

Despite the predominance of negative feelings in the aftermath of care proceedings, it would be misleading to suggest that that is the whole picture. In seven cases perceptions were more positive. Two mothers, for instance, acknowledged the improvement in their parenting skills as a result of statutory intervention, one telling us:

> I'm trying harder now. The court experience shook me up no end and made me wake up.

For this mother placement in a residential unit and the continuing support she derived from this resource, had been 'very helpful' and an essential part of the rehabilitation process. Others were gratified at the extra support or practical resources which had been made available. Some parents described improved relationships with their children and stronger bonds:

> Things are a lot better. I am much closer to the children and they are more loving.

> Towards my child my feelings are even stronger.

while five had found relationships with their extended families had become closer and more supportive.

Moreover, only a minority of parents said that no one within the professional system had been of help to them during the intervention process. Lawyers, perhaps predictably, were the most frequently favourably mentioned in this respect, but the list included voluntary agencies, the Guardian ad Litem, health workers, probation officers, foster parents, a housing officer, the police and the judge. One fortunate mother considered that everyone she had been involved with had been helpful. Surprisingly, given the context, a number of individual social workers were also singled out for praise while one mother at loggerheads with the social worker spoke highly of the team manager.

In view of the importance of the ongoing relationship with the agency, in addition to asking parents generally about sources of support we also asked specifically how they perceived the social workers who had been involved with their case during proceedings. Given the general parental reluctance to accept intervention by Social Services as justified, it is of note that in just over half the cases (13 cases, 52%) parents considered that their dealings with individual social workers had been broadly satisfactory, while in six cases the kindness, fairness or helpfulness of individual workers was cited.

It appears again therefore that perceptions are not entirely determined by the context and that individual examples of good practice do not necessarily go unappreciated.

> She was very good, fair and down to earth. She was promoted jobs and I really missed her.

> She did help me a lot. I felt that she wanted me to keep my child if possible and I was able to talk to her.

Honesty, helpfulness, fairness and sensitivity were highly rated qualities. So too were the abilities to listen to and understand the family's viewpoint and to communicate in a down-to-earth way. Practical help and support together with minor but thoughtful kindnesses also conveyed care and understanding, particularly appreciated at points in the process when parents' already low self-esteem plummeted downwards:

> We had a good rapport with her and she had a good attitude towards us. They often forget you feel so vulnerable and confused.

Such attributes could, on occasion, help to change attitudes, even when the initial encounter had been hostile. Moreover, even when a social worker was personally disliked, some parents were ready to acknowledge positive features in the interaction:

> Personally, I don't like him but he is fair. Maybe my circumstances gave us a poor start but we have a better relationship now and I know he is convinced I really care for my child.

Set against these positive ratings, indeed for the most part their mirror image, were a rather larger number of more negative experiences. Criticised workers were seen to be 'devious', 'cunning' or having 'told lies' rather than honest and straightforward; judgemental and biased rather than open-minded, patronising or ignoring parental viewpoints:

> They lied under oath. They are cunning, devious and powerful.

> They talked down to us all the time. Them and us.

> They treated me like a piece of dirt, making out they care when they don't.

As indicated earlier, personal liking is not a *sine qua non* for a positive evaluation. However, it is undoubtedly true that the chemistry between the parent and an individual social worker is an important factor. A number of parents reported feeling 'stuck' with a worker they felt they simply could not get on with although only three in reality had made a formal request for a change, two of whom were successful. Some of these difficulties focused upon mis-matches of gender, culture, age or experience. It may be, of course, that in some of these family situations the chances of any social worker making headway are pretty slim, whilst in times of strained resources, matching of social worker to client is a fairly unattainable ideal. However, it would be an important indication of a readiness to take parental wishes into consideration if their was evidence of a new worker forging a more constructive relationship in the course of proceedings.[4] Similarly, allocating separate workers for children and adults may be seen as a luxury. However in the six cases where this had happened it was very much welcomed.

Ironically, while some families were desperate to get rid of their social worker, others were disturbed by discontinuity, which made them feel even more unsettled and insecure. Even parents who did not get on particularly well with their worker might prefer someone who knew their case. In all, ten families had new workers in the course of proceedings, some more than one. Parents in general were aware, and sometimes quite understanding, of the reasons for changes in social work personnel. However, discontinuity tended to reinforce other negative attitudes towards the overall level of service provision.

Where would parents turn for help if they experienced difficulties with their children in the future? Such a question was not merely academic since a number of those interviewed had many years of potential child-rearing ahead of them or children still at home.

Social workers, predictably, were not at the top of many lists, indeed six parents said in no circumstances would they want to be in touch with anyone from Social Services ever again. It was therefore surprising that the same number said this was the first agency they would turn to, an indication that at least some constructive working relationships had been established. The fact that foster parents and to a lesser extent residential care staff and even one policeman were also cited as preferred sources of help also suggests some positive aspects of the intervention process.

Six parents said they would turn to a voluntary agency, again usually a reflection of positive recent contacts:

> The Barnados' workers. They are very helpful.

> The NSPCC – they are good listeners and understand how you feel.

It is perhaps ironic that the NSPCC, the only other agency empowered by the Children Act to bring care proceedings and which is still primarily and very publicly identified with 'child-saving'[5] should yet suggest itself to some parents as a more acceptable resource to assist family preservation than Social Services which has a specific remit not only to protect children but to provide services to prevent the need for the court process to be invoked.

Health professionals, of one sort or another, however, were the most frequently cited first choice:

> My GP because she is really supportive.

> My health visitor because I talk to her.

> I would start things off with my psychiatrist.

As far as possible, it was evident, parents would want to steer clear of the statutory system and seek help in quarters from which events might less readily escalate. It is perhaps of some comfort that all but one parent was able to identify at least one source of possible help and had not encountered such negative experiences that in future they would prefer to turn their backs on the whole professional system.

NOTES

[1] De Lissovoy V (1979): 'Towards the definition of an "abuse provoking child"'. *Child Abuse and Neglect*, 3, pp 341–50. Winkel FW; Koppelaar L (1991): 'Rape victims: style of self-presentation and secondary victimisation by the environment'. *Journal of Interpersonal Violence*, 6:1.

[2] Hunt J; Macleod A (forthcoming): *The Best-Laid Plans: the Outcomes of Judicial Decision-Making*. The Stationery Office.

[3] Bullock R; Little M; Milham S (1993): *Going Home*. Dartmouth Press.

[4] See also Cleaver H; Freeman P (1996): 'Child abuse which involves wider kin and family friends' in Bibby P (ed): *Organised Abuse: the Current Debate*. Arena-Ashgate.

[5] Fox-Harding L (1991): *Perspectives in Child Care Policy*. Longman.

9 *Summary and ways forward*

Summary

The research sample

This research has reported the views of 34 parents and other adult relatives involved in 25 cases in which care proceedings were brought under the Children Act. These were drawn from a pool of 83 cases examined as part of a project reviewing the operation of the new legislation.

Compared with the sampling pool, the interview group under-represents families reaching court after only minimal involvement with welfare agencies; in most cases the quality of parenting had been under scrutiny for some considerable time. Sample families also displayed a slightly lower rate of social morbidity than the group overall but most were nonetheless struggling with a range of adverse circumstances: poverty, illness, disability or addiction, violent partnerships and poor childhood experiences.

The pre-court process

Parents brought to court extremely negative views of their contact with the child protection system. The legitimacy of statutory intervention was generally denied, even when some cause for concern was acknowledged. Parents suffering from mental illness and learning difficulties felt particularly unjustly stigmatised at being drawn into a system which labelled them as child abusers.

Services previously offered to families were seen as inconsistent, inadequate or inappropriate, skewed towards a narrow focus upon the child, ignoring the therapeutic needs of parents and the context within which they were struggling to bring up their children. Poor housing, the residue of their own damaging childhood experiences, and above all, the impact of domestic violence, were key issues for parents which they saw as being infrequently adequately addressed by social workers.

Few parents had any sense of having participated in decision-making or having been engaged in partnership with Social Services prior to court action, reporting lack of consultation, inadequate information and feelings of powerlessness. Though welcoming the opportunity to attend case conferences most felt unable to make proper use of this and found the experience confusing, intimidating and demeaning. Estranged fathers and members of the extended family felt especially marginalised at this stage of the process.

Particularly negative views were expressed where court orders had been sought on children who were already accommodated, usually as an alternative to earlier court action. Such parents felt coerced and manipulated into accepting accommodation in the first instance, confused about the subsequent goals, ill-informed about their rights and when court action was later taken, deceived about the agency's intentions.

Even though with hindsight many parents could see that they had been warned that compulsory intervention was a real possibility, most had not taken this on board. The initiation of proceedings came therefore as a great shock, particularly to those whose children were accommodated or where there had been an accumulation of concerns rather than a major incident of abuse.

Court proceedings

The majority of parents were practically, as well as psychologically, ill-prepared for proceedings and voiced a unanimous need for more information: on the physical layout of the courtroom, for example; the personnel involved; the nature of the formal adversarial process and their own role in it; the reasons for the various hearings and the likely duration of the process; the transfer to different courts. Verbal information was rarely supplemented by written material which would have been generally valued.

Levels of apprehension about attending court did not, in the main, substantially diminish with experience. Each hearing therefore reactivated anxiety and distress. This was exacerbated when parents were exposed to public gaze while waiting, often for quite lengthy periods, before their case was called. None the less these parents considered it important to be there and had sometimes overcome considerable practical as well as emotional difficulties in maintaining a high attendance rate.

Inside the courtroom, as well as in the waiting area, parents felt isolated and unsupported. Their physical position in the courtroom both symbolised and actuated an exclusion perpetuated by their lack of understanding of an overly complex and formal process and incomprehension of legal discourse.

Few parents gave oral evidence, reinforcing their perceptions of being marginalised by the process. Those who did found the experience of being in the witness box too intimidating to be able to give of their best, confused by the language of their interrogators, rushed or tricked into giving answers which did not reflect what they really wanted to say. What most parents wanted was to be able to put their view of things directly to the judge or magistrates.

Parents generally welcomed the opportunity to submit written evidence. However there was a widespread perception that this counted for little compared with the professional evidence marshalled against them. Some parents were not aware that they might have been allowed to instruct their own expert and less than half had actually done so. Few called on evidence from lay people who knew their family well but many would have liked to do so, feeling resentful that the court was only getting a partial view of their lives from professionals emphasising their faults.

Despite the requirement to disclose evidence in advance there were still some worrying complaints from parents that they had only seen some statements just prior to a hearing, with insufficient time to absorb them before going into the courtroom. The language in which statements are framed compounds these difficulties, many parents pleading for the elimination of jargon and complex phraseology.

Greatest criticism, however, was reserved for the content of evidence with many accusations of fabrications, exaggerations and distortions. Few parents considered Social Services to have been fair in their presentation of the case against them but most felt powerless to do anything effective about it.

Delay

Universally parents found the period their case was before the court highly stressful. Most considered that proceedings had dragged on too long, amplifying their distress, prolonging insecurity and increasing their difficulties in managing their relationships with separated children.

Professionals in the process

All the parents interviewed were legally represented and most saw representation as crucial. Only two dissatisfied parents would, on another occasion, opt to represent themselves.

Few parents were represented by solicitors with specific expertise in this area of law. The majority, however, were satisfied with the standard of service, the principal complaint being lack of continuity. Highly rated qualities included commitment, a readiness to listen, the ability to advise and explain in straightforward and honest language and a participatory approach which involved the client throughout the process.

Counsel represented parents in almost half of the sample cases. Although these parents had more often lost their case than those using solicitors alone, they nonetheless reported feeling more empowered and levels of satisfaction were high. Apart from the capacity to turn in a good court performance personal characteristics such as warmth and understanding were again highly rated.

The role of the Guardian ad Litem was generally fairly well understood although their partnership with the child's solicitor was not. Most parents were also positive about their contact with the guardian although there were some critical comments and a substantial minority perceived the guardian to be unduly influenced by the local authority.

The majority of parents considered that they had been treated fairly by the judiciary with criticism being fairly mild and quite outweighed by more positive assessments. Highest levels of satisfaction were expressed when judges and magistrates had spoken directly to parents, shown an interest in the family and displayed warmth and understanding.

Parents place a high premium on judicial continuity and dislike change which is perceived as disruptive and time-wasting. They resent the recapping involved, are anxious about new judges getting only a superficial view from reading the papers and fear inconsistency.

Interim placements and contact

Most of the parents in the interview sample were separated from their children for at least part of the proceedings. Almost all the children were looked after or accommodated in foster homes. Few reported being consulted about the choice of placement although this was not usually a source of criticism. Parents reacted positively, however, to being asked about their children's particular special needs and valued this consultation.

Although there were a number of complaints about foster placements almost all were situational: inappropriate ethnic matching, separation of siblings, distance from home, disruption of schooling or friendship groups. Almost all parents spoke positively about the carers themselves.

The majority of parents were dissatisfied with some aspect of their contact – its frequency or duration, for example, the distance they had to travel or the conditions under which it had to take place which exacerbated their own difficulties in dealing with separation. Supervised contact was universally loathed. Only a minority found social workers to be sympathetic to their experience. Rather paradoxically, however, most appeared to be satisfied with the level of control the court exercised over interim contact arrangements.

In contrast many parents, especially those whose children had previously been accommodated, resented the imposition of Interim Care Orders. Even amongst those parents who admitted they might have been tempted to remove, it was reported that the fact of the case being before the court proved sufficient deterrent.

Outcomes

Parents in ten of the sample cases were broadly satisfied with the legal outcome even if they had very mixed feelings about the continued involvement of Social Services in their lives. The remainder reported violent initial reactions of rage and despair, particularly intense among those who appear to have been ill-prepared for the possibility of an adverse decision.

Whatever the result, most were too agitated at the time the court delivered its verdict to take in much of what was being said, in some cases to the extent of not realising what the final order was, although all understood whether they had retained or lost their children. Explanations given in court were clearly not enough, parents need something in writing which they can absorb in less fraught circumstances.

The nature of the outcome did not invariably determine parental views on the fairness of the legal process with parents in five cases with unfavourable outcomes conceding, even if reluctantly, that they had been treated justly by the court.

The aftermath

In the aftermath of care proceedings, whatever their outcome, parents are frequently in a state of emotional turmoil, struggling to come to terms with what has happened and rebuild their lives. Informal sources of support at this stage may be absent because of the condemnation or alienation of the extended family or the local community, while there may be ambivalence or outright hostility to Social Services' continuing role.

Despite general parental denial of the need for court action just over half the parents considered their dealings with individual social workers during proceedings had been broadly satisfactory. Honesty, fairness and sensitivity were highly rated qualities as were the abilities to listen and to communicate in a straightforward way. Such qualities could turn around relationships which had initially been hostile.

Personal chemistry was seen to be an important element in the worker–client relationship. Thus changing a worker, or allocating an adult social worker to a parent could lead to a more positive perception. In general, though, discontinuity was disliked, reinforcing negative attitudes towards the level of service provision.

Parents who needed help with their children in the future would be unlikely to turn to Social Services, preferring to steer clear of the statutory system and turn to health professionals or voluntary agencies.

Ways forward

The parental perspectives recorded in this report, as the foregoing summary makes clear, make somewhat dismal reading. The parity of the experiences reported by parents in this project with those encountered in our previous research suggests that parents subject to care proceedings remain just as disaffected and marginalised under the Children Act as they were before. Indeed most of the parents who had personal experience of proceedings under previous legislation confirmed this.

It would be unrealistic, of course, to think that we could ever create a system in which parents subject to child protection proceedings, particularly those who lose their children, could ever feel totally positive about their experience. This does not mean, however, that changes could not be introduced which would help to make that experience less negative.

There is evidence for this contention in the fact that four sets of parents previously involved with the courts pre-Act *did* consider that the Children Act had improved certain aspects of the process; they spoke approvingly of increased participation in decision-making and negotiation; greater openness and willingness to share information; more respect, consideration or sensitivity shown to them from both practitioners and court staff, and a better chance that children will remain within the family setting. These positive perceptions were reflected in comments such as:

The system is much better, much more fair.

It's good. You are more able to read statements and take part in meetings. There is a more democratic approach.

Further, while on the whole, parental perceptions of the process were closely linked to the outcome, they were not entirely determined by this. As noted in the previous chapter, in five of the 15 cases with unfavourable outcomes parents conceded that they had been treated fairly. Conversely there were also cases where a positive outcome was insufficient to overcome negative perceptions of the process.

Finally, and to our mind most tellingly, there was evidence throughout our research interviews that parents' perceptions were not totally subsumed by their refusal to accept the legitimacy of intervention and that they were, in many instances, operating a fine discrimination. Thus there were examples of parents distinguishing between the system and the practitioners operating the system; comparing the practice of different practitioners; differentiating between liking a social worker and respecting his/her approach. Again and again it was evident that small indicators of respect or concern – a foster parent asking permission to take some action in relation to the child, for instance, a social worker assisting with transport, a judge looking at the family photographs – were of great importance to parents, probably far more than practitioners realise.

We consider therefore that it is not crying for the moon to search for ways in which the experiences of parents caught up in these most distressing events could be improved.

The need for information

The need for parents to be better informed at all stages of the process was a dominant theme in the research. It was evident, for example, that some parents were ignorant about their rights in respect of accommodation, being accompanied at case conferences or the effect of Care Orders; uncertain where to go for legal advice; unclear about most aspects of the legal process and its personnel; uncomprehending of the reasons for court decisions. Practitioners, of course, need to ensure that they are assiduous in providing and reinforcing information and advice. They should not assume that parents will ask, they may not know or be in a position to assess what they need to know about the system. Moreover, one-off explanations are insufficient; in a very distressed state anyone's ability to take in and retain information is limited.

Oral information alone would seem to be insufficient; resources need to be devoted to providing comprehensive and user-friendly written information. The possibility of using other media, such as videos and computer programs, could also usefully be explored as a means of offering more experiential learning. We would suggest that information packs could be developed, in consultation with parents who have experienced care proceedings.

Advice and advocacy

The Children Act has considerably improved parents' formal rights within care proceedings, making them automatic parties entitled to non-means, non-merit tested legal aid. It remains of concern, however, that parents can still be represented by lawyers without accredited expertise in this area of work. Although most parents were satisfied with their lawyer's performance, we would suggest that in this respect they may be insufficiently knowledgeable to make an adequate assessment and that action should be taken to ensure that all lawyers operating in this critical area of work are appropriately qualified.

It is evident, moreover, that as the Children Act has encouraged local authorities to seek to work with parents wherever possible without recourse to court that the locus of decision-making has shifted significantly into the local authority domain. Partnership may be a very laudable ideal, but parents are very unequal partners. Ensuring they have access to an independent source of advice and if necessary advocacy, is an important part in redressing, to some degree, this imbalance. Parents who were accompanied by legal representatives at case conferences, for instance, clearly felt more positively about the experience. Such a service might not necessarily be provided directly by lawyers although if lay people were used they would need access to legal advice.

Empowering parents in this way, we would suggest, might well keep some cases out of court altogether, perhaps by securing provision of appropriate services or mediating between the family and the agency. Where all such efforts are unavailing, then at least one could be more confident that parents had had a fairer deal even if they might not necessarily feel any better about the result.

Clarity of communication

Involvement of a third party in the relationship between parents and agency might also help to overcome one of the primary difficulties reported by parents, the lack of appreciation of the agency's position and intentions before the decision is taken to initiate care proceedings. This is not necessarily a result of any obfuscation by social workers. As noted earlier, with hindsight many parents realised that they had been warned about the possibility of court action but had not taken it seriously. A family advocate might therefore have a useful role in translating agency concerns and encouraging a more appropriate response.

At the same time those involved in the child protection system need to be certain that their messages to parents are clear: about the nature of the concerns, the expectations of change, and the potential outcome if warnings remain unheeded. If this is not done unambiguously, there is a tendency for some parents to put their heads in the sand or to play dangerous games of 'brinkmanship'. When proceedings eventually have to be initiated they are accordingly shocked, often resentful and may feel deceived and betrayed. This is perhaps particularly the case when children have been accommodated.

Indeed the need for practitioners to be open, honest, straightforward and upfront emerged as a theme throughout the research, particularly in relation to social workers and Guardians ad Litem. Such ideals, we acknowledge, may not always be easy to realise, particularly when the initial parental reaction to such clarity may well be anger or extreme distress. Nonetheless, in the long run the consequences of fudging issues and avoiding confrontation are likely to be deleterious.

Addressing parental need

Again and again the parents interviewed in this research identified the need for a readily accessible befriender and confidant(e) who would guide and support them through the court process. Generally none of the professionals already involved in their case was felt to be meeting this need. Although occasionally social workers can do so, in most cases the level of ambivalence if not outright hostility is too great for this not to be problematic. Previous sources of support, such as family support workers, for example, may be compromised by having to give evidence for the local authority case.

We are also concerned that more attention should be paid to parents' needs once proceedings are over. The inadequacy or inappropriateness of the support available to those who had lost their children permanently was most obvious. Frequently it seemed as if parents had been left to cope alone with their grief and loss, cut off from their families, stigmatised in their neighbourhoods, sometimes retreating into depression or addiction. We would urge that some form of independent counselling be made available to families in these circumstances, perhaps through extending the work of post-adoption support services. Apart from the sheer humanitarian justification for such provision, there are pragmatic arguments in terms of the welfare of future children of the family and in the demands likely to be made upon the mental health services.[1]

The needs of parents who retain care of their children is an issue also to be addressed. Such parents may be acutely ambivalent about the continued involvement of Social Services and fearful of admitting to any difficulties lest this jeopardise their position. It may therefore be necessary to bring in some-one free from statutory responsibility for the case, a co-worker perhaps from within Social Services, or a worker from a voluntary agency. Indeed such splitting of the support and child protection roles may enable both to be more adequately exercised. As indicated earlier, in interviewing parents post-proceedings we were often concerned at their denial of the validity of intervention and parental responsibility for lack of care. There is potentially a danger that when workers strive to help parents after court action is concluded the reasons for agency concern become obscured.

Another consistent theme in the interview material was the plea for social workers to take account of the total family situation rather than concentrat-ing exclusively upon child protection issues. The expressed need for greater insight into the impact of domestic violence, which was particularly strong, would seem to indicate there is a pressing need for practitioner training in this area of work.

A rather more complex issue to address is the handling of cases involving mental illness. Such parents felt particularly aggrieved and unjustly stigmat-ised by being labelled as child abusers even though they felt they had not actively or intentionally harmed their children, but defaulted from their responsibilities through incapacity. The system was thus perceived to be unfair and unfeeling towards parents who may be able to care adequately for their children when well. Yet the impact of the acute phase of psychiatric disturbance on the children and the long-term effects of disruptions in care can undeniably result in significant harm.[2]

There are no easy answers to these dilemmas. We can only urge that the management of such cases and the appropriateness of the services available should be carefully evaluated to ensure that all alternatives are fully explored and that the work of child protection and mental health practitioners is well co-ordinated. Sadly, it seems from parents with previous experience of the pre-Act legislation, wardship, which is no longer generally available, may have offered a less stigmatising experience when the authority of the courts was deemed necessary.

Reforming the court process

Although the parents we interviewed mostly questioned the need for the statutory intervention taken, it was notable that they accepted the authority of the court and did not in general consider that they had been treated un-justly. There were, however, many ways in which they considered the court process itself might be improved.

Efforts need to be made to reduce waiting time and minimise delay, since both add to parental distress and fuel their perceptions of an inefficient and uncaring system. Court hearings need to be less intimidatory, less imper-sonal and more participatory. Seating arrangements should enable parents to sit alongside their solicitors and not require them to give evidence from the witness box. Language should be more comprehensible with professionals more sensitive to parents' vulnerability and anxiety, especially when they are giving evidence, allowing them the time to deliver what they want to say. Parents should be allowed to bring a supporter of their own choice into the courtroom, within discretionary limits.

Parents would feel less depersonalised if judges and magistrates introduced themselves, spoke to them directly and explained aspects of the process. Greater continuity among the judges and magistrates hearing a case would be much appreciated as would a clear demonstration that the adjudicator is familiar with the details and is concerned about the family. Most important of all parents wish to participate more directly in proceedings and to present their side of the story in their own words.

The authors' knowledge of other jurisdictions suggests that the qualities these parents sought in the judicial process are probably more in evidence elsewhere. However none of these improvements is dependent upon fundamental change within the court system and many do not even have any resource implications. Some, indeed, may seem trivial. Yet one of the very clear messages from the research was that in the context of a process which is fundamentally demeaning and acutely painful, small kindnesses and individual indications of respect and concern can have a significant effect upon parental perceptions. In an area of work which can be profoundly depressing and where practitioners may feel that there is little they can do as individuals to mitigate the inherent trauma, this finding provides some grounds for qualified optimism.

NOTES

[1] Bowlby J (1983): *Separation, Anxiety and Anger*. Vol II of *Attachment and Loss*. Hogarth Press. Bowlby J (1991): *Loss – Sadness and Depression*. Penguin Psychology.

[2] Cleaver H; Unell I; Aldgate J (1998): *Parents' Problems, Children's Needs. Child Protection and Parental Mental Illness, Problem Alcohol and Drug Use and Domestic Violence*. Report to Department of Health/Social Services Inspectorate.

Bibliography

Abel GG; Becker JV; Mittleman M (1987): 'Self-reported sex crimes of non-incarcerated paraphiliacs'. *Journal of Interpersonal Violence*, Vol 2, pp 3–25.

Aldgate J (1993): 'Respite Care for children: an old remedy in a new package' in Marsh P and Triseliotis J (eds): *Prevention and Reunification in Child Care*. Batsford.

Aldgate J; Tunstill J (1998): *Children in Need*. Research report to Department of Health.

Bebbington A; Miles J (1989): 'The background of children who enter local authority care'. *British Journal of Social Work*, 19, pp 349–68.

Berridge D; Cleaver H (1987): *Foster Home Breakdown*. Blackwell.

Borkowski M; Copner R; Lowe N (1993): *Pathways to Adoption*. HMSO.

Bowlby J (1983): *Separation, Anxiety and Anger*. Vol II of *Attachment and Loss*. Hogarth Press.

Bowlby J (1991): *Loss – Sadness and Depression*. Penguin Psychology.

Brown M; Madge N (1982): *Despite the Welfare State*. Heinemann.

Browne C (1986): *Child Abuse: Parents Speaking. Impressions of Social Workers and the Social Work Process*. Bristol University School of Advanced Urban Studies.

Browne K; Davies C; Stratton P (1988): *Early Prediction and Prevention of Child Abuse*. Wiley.

Bullock R; Little M; Milham S (1993): *Going Home*. Dartmouth Press.

Carlen P (1989): *Women's Imprisonment – a Strategy of Abolition*. University of Keele, Centre for Criminology.

Cheetlam J (ed) (1982): *Social Work and Ethnicity*. NISS Library no 43. Allen & Unwin.

Cleaver H; Freeman P (1995): *Parental Perspectives in Cases of Suspected Child Abuse*. Department of Health Studies in Child Protection. HMSO.

Cleaver H; Freeman P (1996): 'Child abuse which involves wider kin and family friends' in Bibby P (ed): *Organised Abuse: the Current Debate*. Arena-Ashgate.

Cleaver H; Freeman P (1996): 'Suspected child abuse and neglect: are parents' views important?' in Platt D and Shemmings D (eds): *Making Enquiries into Alleged Child Abuse and Neglect. Partnership with Families*. Pennant Professional Books.

Cleaver H; Unell I; Aldgate J (1998): *Parents' Problems, Children's Needs. Child Protection and Parental Mental Illness, Problem Alcohol and Drug Use and Domestic Violence*. Report to Department of Health/Social Services Inspectorate.

Conley PW; Luckasen R; Bouthilet GM (eds) (1992): *The Criminal Justice System and Mental Retardation – Defendants and Victims*. Paul H Brookes Publishing Co, Baltimore.

Corby B (1987): *Working with Child Abuse: Social Work Practice and the Child Abuse System*. OUP.

Cuff EC; Payne GCF (1962): 'Paranoia and the dynamics of exclusion in Perspectives in Sociology'. *Sociometry*, Vol 25.

Dartington Social Research Unit (1995): *Child Protection and Child Abuse: Messages from Research*. Department of Health Studies in Child Protection.

De Lissovoy V (1979): 'Towards the definition of an "abuse provoking child"'. *Child Abuse and Neglect*, 3, pp 341–50.

Department of Health (1989): *The Care of Children: Principles and Practice in Guidance and Regulations*. HMSO.

Department of Health (1989): *An Introduction to the Children Act 1989*. HMSO.

Department of Health (1991): *Working Together Under the Children Act 1989*. HMSO.

Department of Health (1991): *Patterns and Outcomes in Child Placement*. HMSO.

Department of Health (1992): *The Children Act 1989 Court Orders Study*. SSI.

Department of Health/Social Services Inspectorate (1995): *The Challenge of Partnership in Child Protection: Practice Guide*. HMSO.

Department of Health (1995): *Looking after Children: Review of Arrangements for a Child or Young Person looked after by a Local Authority*. HMSO.

Department of Health and Social Security (1985): *Review of Child Care Law: Report to Ministers of an Interdepartmental Working Party*.

Department of Health and Social Security (1985): *Social Work Decisions in Child Care*. HMSO.

Department of Health and Social Security (1988): *Report of the Inquiry into Child Abuse in Cleveland 1987*. Cm 412, HMSO.

Essen J; Wedge P (1986): *Continuities in Childhood Disadvantage*. Gower.

Farmer E; Owen M (1995): *Child Protection Practice: Private Risks and Public Remedies*. HMSO.

Farmer E; Parker R (1991): *Trials and Tribulations: Returning Children from Local Authority Care to their Families*. HMSO.

Feldman et al. (1987): *Children at Risk – the Web of Mental Illness*. Rutgers University Press.

Finkelhor D (ed) (1986): 'Abusers: special topics' in Finkelhor D and Baron L: *A Source Book on Child Sexual Abuse – New Theory and Research*. Sage, Beverley Hills.

Fox-Harding L (1991): *Perspectives in Child Care Policy*. Longman.

Garbarino J; Gilliam S (1980): *Understanding Abusive Families*. Lexington Books.

Gelles RJ (1987): *Family Violence*. (2nd edition). Sage Library of Social Research, California.

Gibbons J; Conroy S; Bell C (1995): *Operating the Child Protection System*. HMSO.

Hague G; Malos E; Dear W (1995): *Against Domestic Violence – Interagency Initiatives*. The Policy Press, School for Policy Studies, University of Bristol.

Hester M; Radford L (1995): *Domestic Violence and Child Care Arrangements in England and Denmark*. The Policy Press, School for Policy Studies, University of Bristol.

Hetherington R (1994): 'Trans-Manche partnerships'. *BAAF Quarterly Review*, Vol 18, no 3.

Hilgendorf L (1980): *Social Workers and Solicitors in Child Care Cases*. Tavistock Institute of Human Relations.

Howe D; Sawbridge P; Hinings D (1992): *Half a Million Women: Mothers who Lose their Children by Adoption*. Penguin.

Hugman R; Phillips N (1994): 'Like bees round the honeypot: social work responses to parents with mental health needs'. *Practice*, Vol 6, no 3.

Hunt J (1993): *Local Authority Wardships before the Children Act: the Baby or the Bathwater?* HMSO.

Hunt J; Macleod A (1993): *Child Protection Proceedings before the Children Act: a Case for Change?* Report to Department of Health.

Hunt J; Macleod A (1999): *The Last Resort: Child Protection, the Courts and the 1989 Children Act*. The Stationery Office.

Hunt J; Macleod A (forthcoming): *The Best-Laid Plans: the Outcomes of Judicial Decision-Making*. The Stationery Office.

Isaac BC; Minty EB; Morrison RM (1986): 'Children in care – the association with mental disorder in the parents'. *British Journal of Social Work*, Vol 16, no 3.

Kadushin A (1972): 'The racial factor in the interview'. *Social Work*, Vol 17, no 3, pp 88–97.

Law Commission (1988): *Family Law: Review of Child Law: Guardianship and Custody*. Law Comm no 172. HMSO.

Lindley B (1994): *On the Receiving End*. Family Rights Group.

London Borough of Brent (1985): *A Child in Trust: Report of the Panel of Inquiry Investigating the Circumstances Surrounding the Death of Jasmine Beckford*. Kingswood Press.

London Borough of Greenwich (1987): *A Child in Mind: Protection of Children in a Responsible Society: Report of the Commission of Inquiry into the Circumstances Surrounding the Death of Kimberley Carlile*.

London Borough of Lambeth (1987): *Whose Child? the Report of the Public Inquiry into the Death of Tyra Henry*.

Madge N (ed) (1983): *Families at Risk*. DHSS.

Malos E; Bullard E (1991): *Custodianship: Caring for Other People's Children*. HMSO.

Masson J; Morton S (1989): 'The use of wardship by local authorities'. *Modern Law Review*, November 1989.

Matza D; Sykes G (1957): 'Techniques of neutralisation: a theory of delinquency'. *American Sociological Review*, 22, pp 664–70.

Mayer J; Timms N (1970): *The Client Speaks: Working-Class Impressions of Casework*. Routledge Kegan Paul.

Mechanic D (1978): *Medical Sociology*. (2nd Edition). Free Press, New York.

Milham S; Bullock R; Hosie K; Haak M (1986): *Lost in Care: the Problems of Maintaining Links between Children in Care and their Families*. Gower.

Milham S; Bullock R; Hosie K; Little M (1989): *Access Disputes in Child Care*. Gower.

Moss P (ed) (1995): *Father Figures: Fathers in the Families of the 1990s*. HMSO.

Murch M (1980): *Justice and Welfare in Divorce*. Sweet and Maxwell.

Murch M; Borkowski M; Copner C; Griew K (1987): *The Overlapping Jurisdiction of Magistrates' Courts and County Courts*. Socio-Legal Centre for Family Studies, University of Bristol.

Murch M; Hunt J; Macleod A (1990): *Representation of the Child in the Civil Courts: Summary and Recommendations to the Department of Health*. Socio-Legal Centre for Family Studies, University of Bristol.

Murch M; Lowe N; Borkowski M; Copner R; Griew K (1993): *Pathways to Adoption*. HMSO.

Murch M; Mills E (1987): *The Length of Care Proceedings*. Socio-Legal Centre for Family Studies, University of Bristol.

Packman J; Hall C (1998): *From Care to Accommodation*. The Stationery Office.

Peckham A (1985): *A Woman in Custody*. Fontana.

Personal Social Services. Confidentiality of Personal Information (1988). LAC (88) 17. DoH.

Plotnikoff J; Woolfson R (1994): *The Timetabling of Interim Care Orders: a Study Carried out on Behalf of the Social Services Inspectorate*. HMSO.

Prosser P (1992): *Child Abuse Investigations: the Families' Perspective*. Commissioned and published by PAIN – Parents Against Injustice.

Quinton D; Rutter M (1988): *Parenting Breakdown: Making and Breaking of Intergenerational Links*. Gower.

Rowe J; Cain H; Hundleby M; Keane A (1984): *Long-Term Foster Care*. Batsford.

Rutter M; Quinton D; Liddle C (1983): 'Parenting in two generations: looking backwards and looking forwards' in Madge N: *Families at Risk*. DHSS.

Scottish Office (1993): *Scotland's Children: Proposals for Child Care Policy and Law*. HMSO.

Social Services Inspectorate (1995): *The Challenge of Partnership in Child Protection*.

Spencer JR; Flin RH (1993): *The Evidence of Children: the Law and the Psychology*. (2nd edition). Blackstone Press.

Stanko E (1988): 'Fear of crime and the myth of the safe home' in Borad A and Yuo K (eds): *Feminist Perspectives on Wife Abuse*. Sage, London.

Stein M; Carey K (1986): *Leaving Care*. Basil Blackwell.

Thoburn J; Lewis A; Shemmings D (1995): *Paternalism or Partnership? Family Involvement in the Child Protection Process*. Department of Health Studies in Child Protection.

Thomas C; Hunt J (1996): *The Case Workloads of the Civil Courts under the Children Act*. Research report. Centre for Socio-Legal Studies, University of Bristol.

Tunnard J (ed) (1994): *Family Group Conferences: a Report Commissioned by the Department of Health*. Family Rights Group/DoH.

Turner S; Sweeney D; Hayes L (1994): *Developments in Community Care for Adults with Learning Disabilities: a Review of 1993/94 Community Care Plans*. University of Manchester.

Wadsworth MEJ (1991): *The Imprint of Time: Childhood History and Adult Life*. Clarendon.

Waterhouse L (1992): *Child Abuse and Child Abusers*. Jessica Kingsley.

Wedge P; Essen J (1982): *Children in Adversity*. Heinemann, London.

Weir A (1994): '"Split decisions": child care: how adult mental health affects children'. *Community Care*, 1.12.94.

Winkel FW; Koppelaar L (1991): 'Rape victims: style of self-presentation and secondary victimisation by the environment'. *Journal of Interpersonal Violence*, 6:1.

Woolf LF (1995): *Access to Justice: Interim Report to the Lord Chancellor on the Civil Justice System in England and Wales.*

Index

Abel and Becker 18
abuse: court action and 26
accommodation:
    child protection strategy and 23
    'enforced' 23, 24, 26
    questioning necessity of 26
    use of 23–6
    voluntary 23
    see also housing
adoption 57
Afro-Caribbean people 63, 64
alcohol 14, 22, 30
Asian families 14
Australia, new ideas from 4

Barnados 46
barristers 50–1
Beckford, Jasmine 22
Browne and Corby 4

Care Orders 57, 62, 75, 76, 77, 78, 93
case conferences:
    intimidating nature 29, 88
    parents' supporters and 29, 93
    parents' involvement in 28–30, 88, 94
    solicitors and 29, 94
child abuse: false accusations claimed 5
child care research 4–5
Child Protection Register 15, 17
children, blaming 19
Children Act 1989:
    accommodation under 23
    court, avoidance of 94
    court proceedings and 5, 34, 42, 45,
        57, 79
    duration of proceedings 10
    effects of 2, 92
    emphases of 1
    ethos of 1
    evidence disclosure and 42
    families' experiences and 3
    family autonomy and 1
    gestation 1

    intervention and 1, 2
    NSPCC and 86
    parents' experiences and 3
    parents' knowledge of 52
    participation 4, 27, 45
    partnership and 4, 27, 45
    Section 17 22
children's homes 62
Cleveland inquiry 1–2, 4, 17
court proceedings:
    accommodation and 23
    adversarial system 33, 41, 48
    advice 94, 95
    anxiety and 35
    befriender 95
    children, separation from 62
    circumstances changing 72
    confusion about 37, 53
    contact and 69–70
    cross-examination 40–1
    delay 57–61, 89, 97
    developments during 75–6
    duration of 10
    entry into 23
    evidence, bringing 41–2
    evidence, challenging 42–4
    evidence, giving 39–41, 43
    families, variety of 15
    hearings, number of 45
    improving 44–7, 97–8
    information about 33–5, 53
    language of 33, 42–3, 78, 97
    legal aid 94
    need for 26–7
    negativity on entering 31
    objectives of Social Services 75
    parents' suggestions for improving
        45–6
    participation in 38, 39, 45
    preparations for 33–5, 87–8
    reports, timing of 42
    significant harm 5–6
    Social Services' evidence 42–4

court proceedings (*cont.*)
    Social Services' objectives 75
    solicitors and 42
    support after 10
    see also following entries and judiciary;
      solicitors
court proceedings, outcome of:
    Care Orders 76, 77, 78
    children returning home 14, 76, 77,
      81
    concealment of 82
    decisions, implementation of 10
    explanations of 79–80
    loss, coming to terms with 81–2
    parents' comprehension of 77–80
    parents' support after 77, 80–6, 91–2,
      95–6
    relatives and 82, 83
    responses to 76–86
courts:
    acoustics 38–9
    attendance rates high 38
    attending, difficulties of 36
    children and 34
    exclusion in 37
    formality of language 45
    isolation in 37
    layout of 33
    microphones 38
    parents' suggestions for improvement
      36
    parents' supporters needed 46
    seating arrangements 38–9, 97
    waiting at 35–6, 45
    witness box 39–41
criminal activity 30
criminal records 16

drugs 14, 20, 22, 30

Emergency Protection Order 14, 26, 29
ethnic minority groups 14, 31, 63–6
extended families 3, 10, 82, 83
    see also relatives

failure to thrive 26
Family Courts Campaign 4
Family Rights Group 3, 46
Family Service Units 46
Farmer and Parker 4
foster homes 62–6

grandmothers 28
Guardians ad Litem:
    confusion about 52–3
    criticisms of 53
    housing and 22
    information given by 33
    parents' perceptions of 52–3
    recommendations of 76
    reports 42
    responsibilities to child 46
    role understood 53

Health, Department of 4, 10
health professionals 86
hospitals 62
housing, poor 6, 22

information:
    independent source of needed 26
    need for better 24–5, 33–5, 53
injuries, repeated minor 26
Interim Care Orders:
    contesting 42
    criticism of 71
    need for 70–2
Interim Contact Orders 69–70
interim placements:
    contact 66–9, 91
    court proceedings and 62
    criticisms 64, 66
    decision-making, participation in 73
    health conditions 62
    home visits 68
    racial/cultural needs 63–6
    religion and 64
    special needs and 63
    types of 62
interviews:
    access difficulties 12–14
    access procedure 11–12
    case files and 9
    consent and 12
    ethical issues 11
    focusing 9
    nature of 10
    preparations of 9
    problems of 10–11, 13–14
    refusals 13, 14
    reluctance 14
    repeat 10
    researcher training 11
    safety of interviewers 11

interviews (*cont.*)
    sample representativeness 14–16, 23
    social workers and 11
    timing of 9–10, 13
    transcription 10
    violence and 11

judiciary:
    continuity 54, 97
    criticisms 53–6
    positive assessments of 56
justice: perceptions of 80

learning difficulties 6, 10, 16
legal aid 94
legislative context 1–2

main study 2, 3, 5, 9–10, 25, 57, 72
Malos and Bullard 4
Matza and Sykes 18
mental illness 6, 10, 14, 16, 17, 19, 20, 60
miscarriages of justice 17
Murch 45

Natural Parent Group 5
neglect, chronic 26
New Zealand, new ideas from 4
Nigerian people 64
NSPCC 46, 86

Orkney 17

Packman and Hall 23
PAIN (Parents Against Injustice) 4–5, 17
parental undertakings 72
parenting:
    assessing 17–20
    criticism of, reaction to 18
    monitoring of 17
    standards of 17
    see also following entry
parents:
    acceptance of some problems 21
    accommodation and 23–6
    advice 94
    agreement to interview 9
    befriender/confidante, need of 21–2, 95
    bias in perceptions 3
    blame, shifting of by 19
    child abuse inflicted on 21
    child, blaming 19
    coercion, feelings of 23–4
    deception, feelings of 24

denial of concerns 17, 18–20, 93, 96
    information, better 24–5, 93–4
    justice, perceptions of 80
    labelling 30–1
    powerlessness, feelings of 25
    reports of, researchers' view 3
    responsibility, acceptance of 20
    scrutiny, duration of 15
    Social Services, attitudes to 20–31
    Social Services, warnings from 27, 62, 95
    stigmatisation 30–1
    support for after proceedings 77, 80–6, 91–2, 95–6
    see also preceding entry
Place of Safety Orders 1
police protection 26
poverty 6
prison 67
Project Advisory Group 10
psychiatric illness see mental illness
public law order 5, 17

relatives:
    carers 70
    increasing role 3
    marginalisation complaints 28
    see also extended families
respite care 22

Scotland, ideas from 4
self-esteem, low 22
sexual abuse 1, 19
significant harm 5–6
Sikh families 14
social exclusion 6
Social Services:
    accusations about 43
    agreement of to study 9
    attitudes to 20–31
    Children Act and 2
    communication, clarity of 94–5
    concerns minimised 17, 18–19, 26
    criticisms of 21, 28, 31, 43, 59, 69, 73–4, 80
    immovability, perceptions of 75
    mixed feelings about 76
    parental participation and 2
    precipitate action 17
    pressures on 22
    resentment of 21
    warnings from 27, 62, 95
    see also following entry

social workers:
    accuracy and 43
    availability of 11–12
    scase conferences and 28
    court information given by 33
    discontinuity of 85
    families' present circumstances and 12
    interviews and 11
    parents' perceptions of individual 83–5
    reports 42, 43
    as scapegoats 19
    statements 43
    study, informed of 9
    see also preceding entry
Socio-Legal Centre 3
solicitors:
    case conferences and 29
    child care experience 48, 94
    children's 51–2
    continuity of 49
    criticism of 25, 49
    family law experience 48, 94
    female preferred 50
    information given by 33
    listening 50
    parents seeking 48

    qualities parents value 49–50
    satisfaction with 49, 83
Statutory Intervention Project 2–3
study:
    background to 1–6
    child care research and 4–5
    elements of 2–3
    focus of 2, 4
    full research team and 3
    influences on 3–5
    research instruments 10–11
    sample size 10
    socio-legal influences 3–4
    see also main study
substance misuse 6, 16, 19 *see also* drugs

Timms 4

violence, domestic 6, 16, 21, 96
voluntary organisations 46, 85–6, 96

Woolf Report 34

Index by Peter Rea